The Complete Guide
to Houseboating

JOHN W. MALO

THE COMPLETE GUIDE TO HOUSEBOATING

MACMILLAN PUBLISHING CO., INC.

NEW YORK

COLLIER MACMILLAN PUBLISHERS

LONDON

ACKNOWLEDGMENTS

Writing a valid book involves a dialogue between
the writer and many others to enhance the objec-
tivity, thoroughness, and credence. Beyond the
experiential scope of the author, this book was
made possible by the many associations listed
in the appendix, government and state agencies,
and old salt friends like John Stavinoga, Ron
Gentzen, and Earl Wobeck.

LIBRARY OF CONGRESS CATALOGING IN PUBLICATION DATA

Malo, John W
    The complete guide to houseboating.

    Includes bibliographies.
    1. House-boats. I. Title.
GV836.M34   797.1'2   73-2122
ISBN 0-02-579300-4

Macmillan Publishing Co., Inc.
866 Third Avenue, New York, N.Y. 10022
Collier-Macmillan Canada Ltd.
First Printing 1974

Printed in the United States of America

Contents

Preface *vii*

1. The Joys of Houseboating 1
2. The Distinctive Craft 7
3. Selecting a Houseboat 19
4. The Lexicon of Houseboating 31
5. Afloat and Underway 39
6. Nautical Rules of the Road 50
7. The Houseboat Ashore and Asea 56
8. Essential and Optional Equipment 71
9. Family and Retirement Houseboating 81
10. The Flotilla of Houseboat Models 94
11. Floating Homes and Trailerable
    Houseboats 119
12. Houseboat Rentals in the Northeast and
    Southeast 134
13. Rentals in the Midwest, Far West, and
    Beyond 140
14. Houseboating Waters in the Northeast 147
15. Southeastern Area of Participation 153
16. Midwestern and South Central Areas'
    Potential for Houseboating 159
17. The Western Area and Beyond
    Our Borders 169
    Appendix 175
    Index 179

Preface

In man's eternal and active search for a challenge there seems to be an affinity for the sea—as there is also for other realms of nature.

Those who prefer the water come by that passion through forces that originated 6,000 years ago, when a maritime civilization emerged on the eastern shore of the Mediterranean; or perhaps even before that, when Neolithic man's first crude boats enabled him to extend his vision beyond the land.

For me, the allure of water began in my native Kansas, where the reservoirs contracted and the creeks ran dry in the summer's heat. The appeal was reenforced in adolescence when I read *Dingbat of Arcady*, by Marguerite Wilkinson, a narrative of a seven-week float down Oregon's Willamette River on a homemade boat with only an open pantry atop the deck, and propelled by oars. This teacher-husband and poet-wife spent the summer drifting with the current, camping, and eating by the riverside the wild and simple foods of field, river, farm, and forest. They met adults and children, each of his own world with romance and tragedy, suspicion and friendship, a deep need for sympathy; all the experiences were set against a backdrop of sun, wind, rain, forest, and flower.

Then too, the joy of being borne on a soft magic current was enhanced by reading *Shantyboat*, by Harlan Hubbard who, with his wife, floated down the Ohio and Mississippi Rivers from Brent, Ohio to New Orleans in the late 1940s. Their leisurely journey on a homemade unpowered raft with a one-room cabin, maneuvering the unwieldy craft, living off the land, enjoying the side feeder creeks, happy with their choice, "thankful to be free from that voluntary slavery which most of us must accept in order to earn a living," sums up the experience, as valid today as it was 30 years ago.

If you have not yet found the motivation to ply the waters in a houseboat, then may this book be your *Dingbat of Arcady*.

Principal Waterways of the United States. Courtesy of U.S. Army

The popular American "get away" syndrome is demonstrated where the elusive moments of solitude are hopefully discovered. (Steury Houseboat)

1

The Joys of Houseboating

Everybody, these days it seems, seeks inner peace, but few know how to achieve it. Too often we live out our days without feeling the therapy of the elements. Rarely do we see, hear, or feel a sudden outburst of nature, a sudden squall, the stinging spray, rolling fog, a cold gray sea. Then comes calmness in the eternal pattern—warm sun, clear sky, the safety of your houseboat, and indifference to the petty annoyances of nature or the landlubber's strife.

Afloat and underway, the houseboat offers an escapee potential, freedom from a compulsive program—the clock and calendar. Your world is the prevailing wind and tide and a limitless sky with bold cloud patterns like giant mobiles on high—all interacting in a choreography that has roots deep within all of us.

From your houseboat deck you observe many varieties of nature's work, especially that only clock of importance—the sun and its rising and setting. Cruising the flat water, feeling the gentle pulse of the engine and the cradle roll of the water, you become sensitive to the constant rhythms of nature, the inexorable procession of time, and you learn of your place in the eternal cycle. This escape from the artificial milieu to the natural, from hardness to softness, from lethargy to action is what houseboating is really like.

Our population patterns being what they are, we often yearn to cop out on the endless, self-shattering regimens. Our world is increasingly marked by the predictable, the commonplace, the safe sure thing. New adventure experiences are rare. Houseboating offers an opportunity for the popular American "get away" syndrome where elusive moments of solitude are hopefully discovered. Whether it be drifting along the pine- and granite-banked lakes of northern parallels, threading the lush tropical rivers of the South, or cruising tremendous water impoundments about the country, the harried skipper and crew will experience natural living, bend to it, and come to terms with it.

With the houseboat under your sea legs, you'll ply historic waters, and the ghosts of the past will share the ride: the French *voyageurs* who opened up the St. Lawrence Seaway, Father Marquette and La-Salle on the Mississippi, the Spanish Conquistadores who touched the white sands at Apalachicola and Pensacola, the pirates who bloodied the waters of the Caribbean, and the gallant sea captains whose battleship victories in the Atlantic led to our independence.

Houseboating is not the only way, but it is one way to enhance that integration with the natural, to enjoy that blessed respite from megalomania, and to stir the body to meaningful exercise. Should you involve family and friends, the pleasures multiply.

Family houseboating in an Aqua-Home includes swimming and a picnic on the beach.

Swinging houseboaters aboard Uniflite's Yacht-Home cruise across the lake for beachcombing and a barbecue.

FAMILY HOUSEBOATING

The houseboat is a versatile craft—it can serve as a weekend lodge, summer retreat, part- or full-time retirement home, a meeting place for cronies, even a mother-in-law apartment, when anchored in front of your waterfront home.

Once you leave the dock, you have, in a sense, already arrived at your destination. The boat offers complete habitation, the scene of activity, self-entertainment, transportation, and a semblance of "back home" style of living. The houseboat, however, is never more animated than when the decks, galley, and pilothouse are filled with youngsters. Dad at the helm busies himself with skippering and ponders his shrewdness: respite from high-speed highways, no frantic search for a motel, meals of his choice, eating when he wishes, roasting corn on the aft deck, the cooling effect of water, breezes that discourage bugs, no fixed destination, and a deep sleep at night. The first mate and program director retreats to the galley to prepare a surprise snack, teen-age daughter climbs the top deck to work on a suntan, while cabin boy son positions himself on the stern deck to troll for fish. If the children are young, don't expect them to stay too long with any one project. Don't worry, though, for there are numerous activities (discussed later) as well as vantage points from which they can enjoy the changing scenic beauty and action on the waterway.

For the family with children of disparate ages, at the day's end, it's a matter of dropping off the teen-age set at the marina for a jukebox concert and taking the younger ones down the line for ice cream sodas, or in a dinghy out to where there's no interference with the bright lights to listen to the night sounds and to watch the sky theater.

In a marina you'll use the power hook-up, but if your craft is equipped with a generator, you can select an anchorage removed from crowds and have enough power to run the refrigerator, electric range, television set, reading lights, and so forth. In short, you're away from it all, but there's no need to forgo the creature comforts of a landlubber.

Clusters of houseboats illustrate a river suburbia on the Mississippi River and a houseboat colony on the Miami River.

No need to get up early, but once up you lounge in your pajamas, sip coffee, watch the sun climb and the bird activity, and listen to the shore sounds—all in complete privacy. Should you decide to rendezvous at some recommended fish hole, you're practically there, and the action starts immediately after breakfast, or before for that matter.

"Togetherness" need not be the trite definition of cynics, nor the foil of TV comedians. A houseboat oriented family cooperatively engaged in outfitting for a cruise; casting off; assisting in the navigation; seeking out ideal waters, a clean beach, or island mooring; then swimming, beachcombing, and camping together, can discover in each other a harmony that will sustain both parents and children for the days ahead.

THE SWINGING HOUSEBOATERS

The swinging set, young executives, and suburbanites have discovered houseboating—they bug out for long weekends, enjoy that luxurious state of being away from crowds and off the hot concrete. The escape is enhanced by such activities as water skiing, snorkeling, scuba diving, barbecuing, beachcombing, fish fries, guitar playing, singing sessions, dancing, or just plain goofing off—working hard at doing nothing.

Houseboating is taking its place among such swinging activities as sports car rallies, dunebuggy racing, trailbiking, canoeing, and horseback riding. The houseboat and its area of operation offers a subtle way of roughing it, communing with forces that have more therapeutic value than the heat lamp or massage parlor.

Houseboats, when clustered in favorable areas, have created a new milieu, the river suburbia, that is devoid of streets and traffic, landscaping, child chauffeuring, and snow shoveling. This new way of life, full-time houseboating in suitable climates, is becoming more and more popular. Instead of a static picture window view, there's a front yard that is freshened daily by two tides, the house ventilated by constant winds, and almost always the horizon and sunrise or sunset are visible. There are no locked doors, burglar alarms, telephone or doorbell sounds in this type of home ownership. After the day's program, it's a pre-dinner drink, a steak broiled on a hibachi, dining to stereo music, watching the news on TV, then curling up with a book for some long-deferred reading.

The river suburbanite can remain anchored at his favorite marina, or can eventually cruise to another haunt, staying there briefly or for a long time and moving again as the spirit indicates. There's no lease to fulfill, no timetable to follow, no "must" destination to hurry to. Always there's the guest list: the grandchildren, Aunt Minnie, a rich uncle, your former boss, and mostly your personal friends—the ones you feel most comfortable with.

HOUSEBOAT PERSONALITIES

There are many people who work from their houseboats—professionals, businessmen, artists, and writers who are fortunate enough to get dockage near the center of things in big cities. Should the office be distant, a bicycle or minibike is often used for adequate transport. These personalities live aboard their houseboats to escape the problems of high-rise apartment living, and to cut down the time wasted in heavy traffic. This ideal pattern of commuting is enjoyed in Chicago, Palm Beach, Miami, Seattle, Washington, New York, San Francisco, and many other places.

2

The Distinctive Craft

The houseboat in the spectrum of motorboats is a kind of cruiser, or motor yacht, designed for living abroad, for plying shallow and protected waters, and for traveling long distances. The early home-built, creaky, and unsightly structures on 55-gallon drums for flotation, illegal today in many areas, gave way to progress as manufacturers embraced space-age materials and know-how along with imaginative design. The emergent houseboat became replete with exciting innovations: light and airy cabins, carpeted and curtained; living quarters with ample head-room; picture windows and glass doors; nonskid catwalks and decks; modern heads, including shower, mirror, and vanity; efficient galleys; and pilothouses with instrument panel to control lighting and the various optional power plants.

One need not be an engineer or designer to realize that elaborate living quarters in a craft must come at the expense of desired stream-lining. Consequently, the high-wetted surfaces, speed-length ratio, and lack of chine causes the houseboat to plow the water, throw spray, and suffer less maneuverability in strong winds, tides, and currents. Thus, eye appeal and speed and control are sacrificed for utility and livability —which the owner realizes and accepts.

In the engineering and construction of more expensive models, manufacturers strive to get cruiser qualities into their craft: modified hulls, powerful engines, low-slung superstructures, elaborate appointments, and the like. At the upper half of the scale, a dream houseboat will cost upwards of $50,000 and include a length of 45 feet, beam of 18 feet, an elevated pilothouse that flows into a lounge area, a main deck

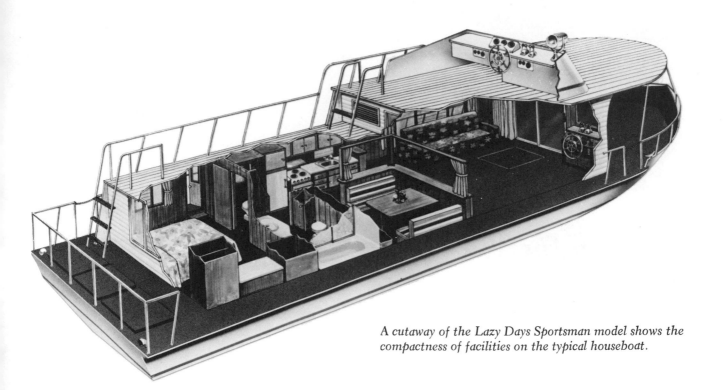

A cutaway of the Lazy Days Sportsman model shows the compactness of facilities on the typical houseboat.

with two staterooms, two baths, and a galley-dining area; louvered safety glass windows with aluminum frames, perhaps thermopane, double thickness for insulation; walk-around decks with railings of anodized aluminum or stainless steel; capacity for 500 gallons of fresh water and 500 gallons of fuel for a pair of engines. Many other luxury items, akin to those in a well-appointed home, are standard equipment and are included in the price.

The houseboat adopts and benefits from travel trailers and mobile homes. None of their innovations in floor plan, construction materials, decor, or furnishings is overlooked by the houseboat designer. Indicative of the plush furnishings available for houseboat interiors are such items as sliding picture windows, drapery, carpeting, pictures, storage space, hanging closets, gas stove with oven, hood, and exhaust blower, sink and counter space, refrigerator, air conditioner, barbecue grill or hibachi, and so on.

SOME PRELIMINARY HOUSEBOAT REQUISITES

David D. Beach, a national boat expert, has been involved in the design and construction of custom and production houseboats for over 20 years. He indicates his requirements of a houseboat as follows:

A floating structure that has livability afloat as its main objective. It adopts the characteristics of a modest apartment and utilizes to the best advantage space offered by the fore and aft decks and the roof.

Trojan aft and guest staterooms indicate how houseboat designers cater to the distaff side of the crew.

The interior areas should be of ample size to accommodate:

A complete culinary facility;

A complete bathroom whose fixtures include a head separate from shower stall or tub, and vanity with mirror;

Complete privacy for those living aboard: for two couples if the boat sleeps four;

Adequate space for daytime living, even though it may have a secondary, converted application, as emergency sleeping quarters (from *Motor Boating & Sailing*, January, 1970).

Alluding to the mobile home again, anyone acquainted with them realizes the extent of comfortable living quarters possible in a limited area. The houseboat also efficiently utilizes every available space; the compact galley, clothes-hanging closets and lockers, assorted storage lockers, and drawers throughout the boat offer a place for everything and keep housekeeping effort at a minimum. Convertible lounges in the cabin, dinette, and pilothouse quickly unfold at bedtime to offer an assortment of sleeping spaces that allow for quite a guest list. And, if the crew gets too large, there are the decks where sleeping bags can be spread.

It is in the interior planning that designers cater to the distaff side of the crew. As homes present an opportunity for the lady of the house to exploit her talents in furnishings and decor, so too, in the houseboat; its color schemes, carpeting, drapery, light fixures, pictures, and perhaps wild cushions, gaudy bean bag seats, and the like can also reflect her creativity.

VERSATILITY AFLOAT AND ECONOMICAL LIVING

The low draft and riding high in the water of most houseboats permit them to travel in only 6 inches of water, which makes possible cruising in places most other motorboats dare not go. The substantial hull permits running up on a beach, island, or sandbar for that break in cruising, whether it be for swimming, exploring, building a beach campfire, or spending the night. The next morning you untie the line, back off the sand, and take off. Specialized equipment for boats is bought to pursue such activities as deep-sea fishing, long-distance cruising, water skiing, scuba diving, or treasure hunting; yet almost any houseboat can be used for these activities.

The economic advantages of extended houseboat living are quite evident. Your rent is reasonable; dockage fees on the average cost a dollar per foot (boat length) per month. Utility bills are commensurate with landlubber rates, and as for taxes, there are none—you only need an annual boat registration, the cost of which varies from state to state, and is scaled according to engine horsepower.

If your neighbors prove incompatible, move to a more desirable spot by heading for the sea or inland waterway, there to seek out another marina, an island, or remote shore. The move doesn't require the packing of luggage, shutting off the water, locking up the house, or notifying the milkman.

The houseboating family, with or without children, learns a less formal, more organized way of life. The youngsters, instead of playing on the street, can go fishing, snorkeling, crabbing, rowing, or building castles in the sand.

Above all, you learn to live with fewer material things, and if you don't think you're materialistic, a great amasser of things, just look at your garage—filled with everything but your car.

For environment-sensitive souls concerned about the houseboat being disruptive to the water and land, they can be relieved by the fact that boating, under prudent control, is harmless to the ecosystems involved. Any number of craft can ride a watercourse with little damage to it, and such associated activities as swimming, skiing, or snorkeling are also without a threat potential. The true houseboater, however, cannot vouch for the minority goof who dumps garbage from his boat and litters beaches, islands, and every shore he touches.

Mothers capture some sun on board a Hobo, while their sons explore underwater things from the aft deck.

HOUSEBOAT USES AND ACTIVITIES

The scope of uses, activities, and new experiences that are possible with the houseboat is without bounds to the imaginative, curious, and active participant. The houseboat can be a floating church, a bank, a facility for a wedding reception, a deep-sea fishing boat, and a craft supreme for water, beach, and island activities. And in our nation's capital, during special events, houseboats anchored in the nearby Potomac River have served to alleviate the housing shortage.

The Floating Chapel is a new concept in an ever-changing ministry. Since 1968 a leisure ministry program has been serving the northland. Piloted by seminary students, the Floating Chapel serves the Eagle River Chain of Lakes area (Wisconsin) providing campfire sing-alongs, activities for youth in local camps, guitar masses, and a number of contemporary Sunday worship services. The Floating Chapel is sponsored by the Pioneer Lake Lutheran Church in Conover, Wisconsin.

The Houseboat Bank. A branch of the Security National Bank, serving vacationers on Long Island, New York, is a houseboat. The skipper is the bank manager, and the first mate is a woman teller. The 34-foot Chris-Craft Aqua Home is equipped with bulletproof glass and is the first houseboat bank in the Northeast.

The idea of a cruising bank came from a bank official while vacation-

Leaving Marina Del Rey in Los Angeles, the Uniflite Yacht-Home serves adequately for a wedding reception. Note the negligible effect of the load on the vessel's freeboard.

ing in the area. He found himself short of money and unable to cash a check. As a result, the houseboat bank, with its interior decor of ship prints and captain's chairs, came into being and serves several communities on a regular schedule during the warm months. At Cherry Grove the port window is used as a walk-up window, complete with deposit and withdrawal slips, loan application forms, and all standard bank services. Vacationers and permanent residents are pleased to have a bank come to them.

A Wedding Reception Aboard a Houseboat is possible, and it has been done, which proves that the houseboat is roomy and stable enough to withstand the festivities involved. A 36-foot-long Yacht-Home with private stateroom and entertainment area, 16 by 10 feet, a convertible dinette, and a forward deck with permanent seats, protected by a canopy, offers a sophisticated facility for bride and groom and guests. And 30 celebrants do not affect the trim of the boat—that is, until the polkas are danced.

Herbert Hoover enjoyed many retirement years houseboating on the Gulf of Mexico off Key Largo, Florida. As a lifelong angler, who had written on the peace potential of fishing, Mr. Hoover was able to continue his love, taking to the waters at every opportunity in his twilight years. Once he was involved in an act of mercy, aiding a distressed vessel in rough waters with little regard for his own safety, and never reported the incident.

President Richard M. Nixon escapes the pressures of his office, in brief respites, by boarding the houseboat Coco Lobo and cruising the waters of Biscayne Bay that border his bayside villa at Key Biscayne, Florida. Piloting the craft from the flying bridge where the views are long and peaceful, the President finds the Secret Service man below does not infringe on the contemplative and rejuvenating cruise.

Big-City Cruising (Chicago, Illinois). If you believe that houseboating is restricted to distant waters, you don't know of the match between the houseboat and the big city. In Chicago the houseboater can cruise the Chicago River past such skyscrapers as the Sears Tower, Marina City, Wrigley Building, Tribune Tower, and Sun-Times veranda, under the bridges of boulevards, and past the site of Ft. Dearborn where the city began. Then the houseboat skipper can cruise into Lake Michigan, heading south to the harbors that berth ocean-going liners or northward to the tree-fringed Northshore. From the shadows of skyscrapers to the open lake of coho salmon fishing describes the range of cruising possibilities in or near the Windy City.

New York City houseboaters are endowed with the Hudson and East Rivers, which afford the unique experience of being able to look up from water level to the spectacular and continuous views of man-made creation. Circling the small island, with a shoreline that thrusts vertically like organized mountain cliffs, one views the many outlets to the Atlantic Ocean, where piers and wharves are crowded with ocean liners and freighters. Other branches of the waterway offer different views of the city: green parks, old houses and gardens off Sutton Place, and playgrounds with children and bridges with traffic giving an animation to the whole experience—houseboating in a megalopolis.

Miami, Florida has a river by the same name. It meanders (from sea-ward) along palm-shaded banks through the heart of the city, with its bustling sidewalk pace, downtown skyscrapers, superhighway bridges, and industrial complexes. Then northwestward you become hemmed in by tropical vegetation which softens and quiets the shoreline. Above and below Just Island you'll find houseboat service facilities, storm-sheltered docks, and charters. Your craft blends in with pleasure and commercial boats, some local, others from exotic places. Leaving the river, you can cruise north along the Intercoastal Waterway and enjoy the "Venice of America," stretching between Miami and Palm Beach.

Seattle, Washington. The houseboat has graced the waterfront of Seattle for 50 years. Puget Sound, the gateway to the Pacific, is filled with pine-covered habitable islands and many sheltered harbors. Along this waterway, the houseboat associates with the numerous fishing fleets. And not unlike the commercial fisherman, the houseboater relishes the battle with fighting Pacific Ocean salmon. On the inland tack the skipper and crew enjoy different experiences, like locking through the Chittendon Locks, then cruising to Salmon Bay, Lake Washington Ship Canal, Lake Union, Portage Bay, and into Lake Washington. There's also an international flair to Seattle waters: the province of British Columbia lies north across the strait, and the Juan de Fuca archipelago to the northwest.

Gunkholing. The houseboater can capture an independence and free-dom that is difficult to find these days. His shallow-draft boat is ideal for gunkholing, the sport of loafing in isolation, sometimes actively, other times passively. First, you leave the crowded marina and heavily plied waters on prescribed routes, then search out a remote cove, bay, or creek. Sometimes these havens can be found near big cities. With the anchor dropped, you sit on the deck, sipping a cool drink, as the feeling of suspended time takes over and you wonder if you are alone in the world. Other houseboaters enjoy observing and photographing wildlife, studying various land formations, and searching out historical sites.

In Arizona the gunkholer probes the cliff-lined, box canyon coves of Lake Powell; in Florida waters the search for serenity ends at a palm-fringed bank; along the Mississippi one finds a back-off with water birds and broad expanses of water lilies. Active gunkholers in the Gulf of Mexico anchor near reefs for fishing, in the Caribbean they search for traces of the colorful buccaneer, and along the Atlantic Coast they gather driftwood and watch the flocks of migrating birds. The sport of gunkholing can be as restful or exciting, as simple or profound as you wish it to be.

Scuba Diving and Snorkeling open up an underwater world, the realm of marine creatures, and they don't spook as you swim by taking in the fascinating views of schools of iridescent fish, waving grass, rippled sand, and filtered sunlight. First there's snorkeling with simple equip-ment, including mask, goggles, air tube, and flippers. You swim along on the surface of the water and view the underwater world, then surface dive when something on the bottom intrigues you. Scuba (Self-Con-tained Underwater Breathing Apparatus) diving requires expensive

Gunkholing helps to capture elusive joys like low-key fishing from a
Steury and a quiet game of checkers aboard a Sylvan.

equipment including a mask and air cylinders with hoses and valves, harness, and flippers.

Most waters offer a visual treat beneath the surface, a little known world of beauty, movement, and mystery. The warm sea near Pensacola, Florida, offers the opportunity of spear fishing near sunken caves and canyons in aquamarine waters. The quarry includes barracuda, grouper, snappers, and flounder. The waters near Santa Rosa Island are rich in the lore of Spanish history, and to this day give up gold coins and numerous other pirate objects. If scouting around old sunken ships is your thing, you'll find modern ones in Gulf waters too, like the battleship USS Massachusetts, an old Coast Guard ship, or a Russian freighter. The string of Florida Keys and the broad expanse of the Caribbean Sea add up to a year-round paradise for the scuba diver.

Fishing is an activity ideally suited to the houseboat. The range of participation is adequate, and the tackle runs the gamut from a simple dropline and hook to deep-sea proportions: strong lines, heavy reels, short rods, and a swivel chair on the stern deck. Outriggers are included too if bill fishing is on the program. The flying bridge is very practical for the spotting of surface-feeding fish, as you try to decoy them with trolling ballyhoo or surface lures. The skipper who loves fishing will have aboard a fish locator, heavy rod, reel and terminal tackle, an assortment of lures and bait—as mullet, squid, and shrimp—and a dip net with a long handle and/or a fish gaff to lift the fish over the gunwales.

Hunting. The houseboat extends the range and increases the success odds of the hunter. An auxiliary boat towed astern or carried topsides enables you to get to weedy and shallow waters, and if your quarry is moose or migratory fowl, that's where they should be. The houseboat serves as a base camp from which the hunter goes to where the game hopefully abounds.

Locating coins and other lost treasures from sunken ships is made easier with White's metal-mineral detector that operates under water.

ABOVE: *Three generations of males still-fishing among the lily pads from a Kayot pontoon boat.* BELOW: *Water skiing is possible behind a Hobo houseboat that speeds and planes effectively.*

Star gazing. This ancient pastime of regarding the sky, its planets, stars and star clusters, and their orbits can be pursued with the naked eye from the deck of a houseboat. The sparkling and twinkling stars are screened out for most people who live in artificially lighted neighborhoods, the luminescence of which dims the celestial sphere.

The evidences of our neighbors in space are a joy to behold, and with an elementary handbook and simple chart, the mysteries clear up a bit, but deepen too. You discover, as did the cavemen, ancient mariners, Columbus, and present-day astronauts, that the planets do not twinkle; they are our nearest neighbors and therefore visible to the naked eye. They are Jupiter, Saturn, Mars, and Venus—which at certain times of the year is bright enough to cast a shadow on earth.

Star gazing is best done on a clear evening when the moon is in its dark phase. Binoculars make it possible to see many stars that are invisible to the naked eye. A flashlight with a concentrated beam can be used by the expert in the crew to point out individual stars and constellations.

The topmost deck of a houseboat, with a clear view of the northern and eastern sky, is an ideal lookout. The star chart—indicating position of stars, planets, and constellations by months and days—should be placed in the pilothouse for handy reference when star gazing is on the program.

Competitive Houseboating. If you're a sea rover bent on rugged competition, you can consider the skipper of the Drift-R-Cruz, who raced his houseboat in the Bahamas 500-mile marathon, or the skipper who piloted his Chris-Craft Aqua Home for 2,000 miles from San Diego to Acapulco, Mexico, and cross the Atlantic from Miami to Nassau.

If you're not so rugged, try the Cross-Florida Boat-A-Cade, an annual October event, from Stuart through the Okeechobee Waterway to Ft. Myers. The rendezvous for the group cruise is at Jensen Beach, where a dinner and dance is held for all participants before departure. The flotilla is escorted by the U.S. Coast Guard Auxiliary and Federal Marine Patrol, and there are three group dinners during the cruise.

Water Skiing is possible if your houseboat can maintain a speed of 18 mph. After the original outlay of money for skis, towline, and ski belt, there's no upkeep involved in this exciting sport, which offers a challenge to the young bloods in the crew.

The Overnight Trip in heavily used waters can be a problem. Areas where you are allowed to land, tie up, and camp, or anchor for the night, are not as extensive as the literature indicates. Your best bet is to patronize a licensed marina. Ft. Lauderdale and Clearwater, Florida, for example, have laws that specify that you may not tie up on property within the city without permission, and also that you may not stay on a boat for more than 6 hours at your own dock, or a friend's. Tying up at a dock at your home is acceptable as long as you do not stay on the boat while it is tied up. The small, isolated, and uninhabited islands located on the waterways within the city limits are also off limits. In all the high-density boating areas, a licensed marina is the only place to be legally docked.

3

Selecting a Houseboat

If you're reading boating magazines, hanging around the waterfront at every leisure moment, and dreaming of far-off places—then you're ready to rent or buy a houseboat.

Houseboaters enjoy the best in boating; they get more boat size value per dollar than most others. They are practical people who use their craft by interweaving the residential, recreation, and transportation aspects to good advantage. For these reasons, the houseboat in the recreation market is coming on strong. It is getting a bigger share of the boat loans in the United States—exceeded only by the number of loans for homes and autos.

GAINING HOUSEBOAT SAVVY

First, go to your local library and survey the boating book and magazine offerings. Subscribe to or buy the publications that give space to houseboating. Study the advertisements, write for literature, amass a file of information: models, engines, accessories, prices, and so on. You will probably soon realize that your ambitions and desires will become attuned to reasonable demands in boat size, power, and price.

Examine the eligible-for-your-needs models by visiting dealers and marinas. Talk to owners of boats to see if they're satisfied and proud enough to show off their craft. Listen to their experiences, joys, and gripes. Attend the boat and outdoor shows that are staged during the winter and spring in most large cities.

FLOOR PLAN
Composite of several houseboat models

BOW

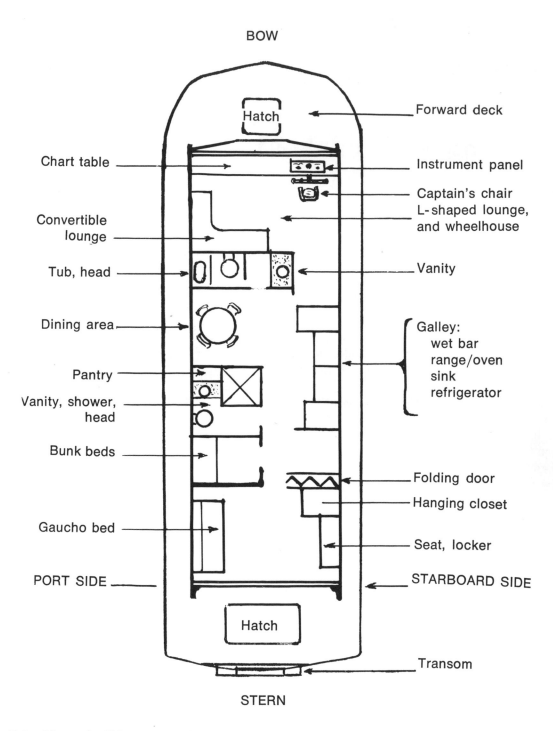

Hatch — Forward deck

Chart table — Instrument panel

Captain's chair
L-shaped lounge,
and wheelhouse

Convertible
lounge

Tub, head — Vanity

Dining area

Galley:
wet bar
range/oven
sink
refrigerator

Pantry

Vanity, shower,
head

Bunk beds

Folding door

Hanging closet

Gaucho bed

Seat, locker

PORT SIDE — STARBOARD SIDE

Hatch

Transom

STERN

Note: These facilities are generally on one or more levels.
Windows, sliding doors, carpeting, shelving—not shown.

Floor plan is a composite of several houseboat models.

The boat purchase is not like buying a suit of clothes or an automobile, but more comparable to buying a house. Guard against the desire to buy a houseboat that is over-sized, over-powered, and over-priced. After all, a pleasant experience, guesting on a friend's houseboat, is no reason to dash out and buy a 50-footer. If possible, first rent the model that interests you. Check its behavior in choppy waters, crossing the surge of wakes from large boats, and if she lacks stability, you've picked one suitable only for sheltered waters. The houseboat design that calls for a flat barge hull, or pontoons, is not ideal for open-water cruising. These serve adequately in sheltered waters and when conditions are ideal. However, the retiree who is not concerned with schedules and picks out the best weather days for going asea is little concerned with this disadvantage. He cruises at a leisurely pace of 8 to 10 knots and enjoys the scenery, along with the low fuel bills.

Be assured that there is no perfect houseboat. The craft for you is wrapped up in your personal requirements; it may be right for the junior executive, swinging bachelor, or a father of six in a given season or perhaps for many years. The requirements of the owner may be completely filled, but those requirements can change, and the houseboat will be replaced.

Trading up is a traditional and happy part of the boating game. The odds indicate that the boat owner will sell his first model, and buy a new one with more features in design, bigger horsepower engine and props, and the female influence will prevail in more living space, adequate powder room, and improved decor.

In order to make the first boat acquisition more valid, visualize present-against-future needs, your financial outlook, what the boat will be used for, areas of participation, and the required sleeping accommodations.

Houseboat Checklist. In summary, the ideal houseboat should be fast enough to outrun oncoming storms and to move to and from destinations when fishing, visiting, refueling, or whatever. Your houseboat should respond well to the helm and give a comfortable ride. The craft should be safe and able to withstand pounding waves without damage to hull, fuel tanks, and seams. It should be fitted with adequate power navigational instruments and safety equipment.

SOME BACKGROUND NOTES

The houseboat was mostly a custom-built (and expensive) deal in the 1940s and 1950s. Since then, this specialized craft has come on strong, the sales rising from 500 to over 4,000 units per year in the past decade. As there were few preconceived positives that dictated design, construction, and the like, manufacturers made the most of modern materials and imaginative design to evolve the better designed, more efficient, and better houseboat.

In overall appearance, the designers had to grapple with the monotonous similarity in most houseboats. In the 1940s when you'd seen

The Watercraft model illustrates the traditional flat-bottom hull that affords maximum interior space.

the inside of one boat, you'd seen them all: the head, tables, galley, and dinette were in predictable juxtaposition. The subsequent individuality in interiors probably indicates that more women were brought into the designing. In the burgeoning industry, specialized houseboats were manufactured to meet specific conditions and needs, and price-wise they were cheaper than cruisers of the same size. The houseboat boom was launched, but not without problems.

As is often usual with a potential bonanza enterprise, irresponsible boat builders suddenly boarded the houseboat bandwagon. Several were fly-by-night operators, others back-yard and garage builders, and though a minority in the field, their irresponsible presence hurt, and this soon led to reform.

In 1966, reputable and concerned manufacturers formed the International Houseboat Manufacturer's Association. In 1967, with the encouragement and cooperation of the Boating Industry Association, the houseboat industry really took off. The group immediately established a houseboat engineering standards program, and the shanty boat era was ended.

The men responsible for the "new look" in houseboating included: Pete Ball of Chris-Craft; Dick Brooks, Carri-Craft; Tom Bastis, Boatel; Jack Byquist, Holiday Mansion; Don Echols, MonArk; Seabury McGowan, Uniflite; Glen Nichols, Sea Going; Russ James, Nauta-Line; Jack Seastrom, Kenner; Dick Peterson, River Queen; Dick Whittaker, Whitcraft; and Paul Hadley, writer and former president of the association.

HULL TYPES AND CONSTRUCTION

Houseboat hulls come in many variations of three basic forms: the flat bottom, round bottom, and shallow V-shape bottom. The traditional houseboat uses the flat-bottom hull. It is the least expensive to build and offers a good foundation upon which to construct a superstructure that affords maximum interior space, riding stability, and comfort. The rectangular boxy hull, however, displaces water as it plows through it, and stability suffers in rough waters and strong winds.

Other houseboat hulls are constructed with round and V-shaped bottoms. They offer a fast and comfortable ride, but are expensive to construct. These sophisticated hull designs combine the contoured lines forward with a flat planning area aft. An adequate power plant pushing the modified hull gives a smooth ride at either slow or high speeds, in a chop, or on calm water. At increasing speeds, the houseboat planes very much in the manner of a cruiser or yacht.

Hull Construction should be of material that offers adequate overall strength, durability at the joints and seams, and a minimum of maintenance. Such materials include wood, fiberglass, aluminum, and steel. A survey, by the author, of 128 houseboats indicated the following types of hull construction:

Houseboat hull with a V-shape bottom is pushed by a powerful Merc outboard.

Fiberglass	59
Aluminum	41
Steel	24
Wood	4

This tally seems to be typical of the trade today.

Wood Hull construction utilizes conventional planking, lapstrake, and sheet or molded plywood. Wood construction offers a hull of durability and low cost. Old salts consider nothing but wood, because of its availability, shaping characteristics, and ease of repair. On the other hand, the expense of incorporating wood properly in design, the cost of competent craftsmen, and the required subsequent care convince most manufacturers to consider other materials.

Fiberglass, utilizing glass fiber cloth and adhesive resins for bonding, is capable of being molded into many types of durable boat shapes. The material requires little painting, patching, or maintenance. Its flexing properties enable the hull to receive lateral and bottom impact without injury to the skin.

Aluminum, as hull material, is lightweight and tough and in the finished product requires less engine power to be efficiently and quickly moved. It is easily shaped, and various sections are readily riveted into place. Marine-grade aluminum, resistant to corrosion, is used by most manufacturers. For major repairs, a problem exists, in that qualified aluminum welders are scarce. Aluminum's high tensile strength and its ability to be stretched and formed are the attributes that interest the houseboat builder and user.

Steel is the strongest material for hull construction, and many houseboaters driving over shallow water, hearing the crunchy sound of rock and coral and coming through with unscathed hull, swear by this material. The most expensive of materials, it offers joints and seams of 100 percent strength with watertight bulkheads and is generally leak- and distortion-proof.

In summary, there is no single answer as to which material is superior. Regardless of material, a houseboat bought from a reputable company will be basically seaworthy and worth the price because of tailored construction to a proven design and excellent workmanship.

Hazard of Electrolytic Damage. Metal hulls of aluminum and steel require electrolysis detectors to prevent, or rather bypass, the damaging electrolytic action which can occur in the electrical imbalance of metals in a water solution that carries the electric current from one point to another. In the ion exchange, there is a breakdown of metal, actual disintegration into the solution, very much as in the process of electroplating. The metal hull breaks down, characterized first by small pit holes, then further and deeper disintegration. Specialized paint can help control the problem, but electrolysis-control devices, available commercially, are best. The antifouling system includes two anodes of zinc or magnesium which are attached to the keel near the motor fittings. The strong electrical charges attack the anodes and spare loss to the hull or fittings. Many houseboats anchored in a saltwater marina, with a minimum of water movement, can produce a very potent solution that speeds up the action of electrolytic damage.

POWERING THE HOUSEBOAT

Houseboats are propeller driven, powered mainly by three types of engines: the outboard motor; the inboard engine coupled to an outboard drive (I/O) called stern-drive; the inboard installation, an engine linked to a fixed drive shaft and propeller.

The Outboard Motor is excellently engineered, with ignition-key starting, pushbutton shifting, single-lever remote control, effective silencing and exhaust systems all encased in stylish and streamlined covers. The horsepower ratings are upgraded almost annually and provide all the thrust needed to move the houseboat adequately. Portability is a great advantage of the outboard. A balky motor can often be repaired while in the water, but one needing an overhaul can be removed from the transom and wheeled to the repair bench. It can be replaced by a "loaner" if power is needed immediately.

A second outboard engine of light weight and low horsepower can be mounted to one side of the big outboard, to be used for slow-speed fishing and for emergency propulsion should the main engine fail.

The Inboard-Outboard Engine is a combination of inboard and outboard concepts; it consists of an inboard engine (automobile) placed within the craft and coupled through the transom to an outboard-type drive unit, called an outdrive. This unit reacts faster and easier than fixed propeller systems. The entire outdrive is electrically powered which enables you to automatically raise or lower the drive unit. This is very important when cruising in shallow water, beaching the craft, or when clearing a weed-fouled propeller, or replacing a battered one.

Twin motors offer a safety factor in quick turning and stopping and afford slow-speed maneuverability in close quarters, in shallow, tricky waters, and when docking or undocking.

The Inboard Engine is an automobile engine, manufactured and modified for marine use. It is placed forward of the transom with a straight propeller shaft connected directly to the marine transmission which is mounted at the rear of the engine itself. The cooling system is modified to draw upon the surrounding water instead of utilizing a closed, recirculating system as in an automobile.

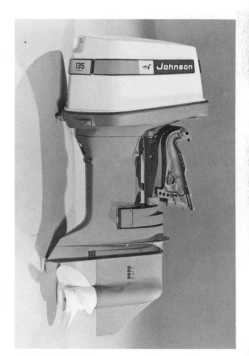

150-HP MERCURY 1500

135-HP JOHNSON SEA HORSE

The Big Three in outboard motors! Each has something for which it can be highly recommended.

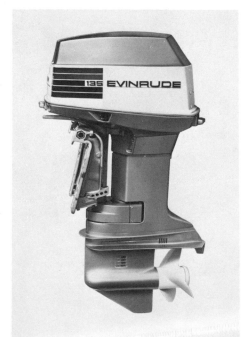

135-HP EVINRUDE STARFLITE

For shifting, the inboard has only one forward gear, a neutral position, and a reverse gear, which also acts as the braking system. The inboard engine horsepower range is great, but the 190- to 225-horsepower range seems to be most popular.

One disadvantage of the inboard is the vulnerability of the exposed long shaft to underwater obstacles. A bent shaft requires a drydock repair.

The Inboard Diesel Engine is simpler than its gasoline counterpart; it is more economical on fuel, the carburetor and spark plugs are unnecessary, there are fewer parts, and hence it requires less maintenance. The diesel engine, however, costs more because its construction is more rugged, component parts are heavy, and the complete engine is large. These factors indicate why the diesel is used more for commercial boats and motor yachts than for pleasure boats.

The adaptation of the automobile engine to marine use makes the garage mechanic very happy for he can troubleshoot many of the problems.

Engine Control comes from the pilothouse which is generally aft of the bow deck and contains the wheel, compass, engine controls, and table space for charts. An instrument panel may have lights or needle indicators to warn of the operation of various systems: temperature, oil pressure, electrical, fuel, and so on.

The more expensive houseboats include a second wheel or auxiliary control center atop the cabin, a flying bridge as seen in deep-sea fishing craft. The remote engine controls are often upright levers, pushed forward to proceed, pulled back to reverse, and set upright for neutral.

A sea gull's view is possible for this couple from a flying bridge of a Harbor House houseboat.

Once the engine gears are engaged, the lever serves as a throttle. The elevated position of the flying bridge gives the skipper and crew an unobstructed view of the course from this breezy and sporty vantage point.

Adequate power is necessary for proper engine and instrumentation operation, lighting, and heating. Two sets of electrics are recommended: one to work off the boat's batteries (a pair of 12-volt), the other system to be 110-volt power capable of hooking up to marina outlets or to the boat's own generating plant. These standards assure electrical output adequate for lights, heaters, refrigerator, toaster, navigational equipment, and galley.

THE USED HOUSEBOAT

There are few bargain houseboats! Unless you are a mechanic and an experienced boater, the best way to discover "a steal" is to hire a naval architect or marine surveyor to thoroughly check out the craft in question. He is trained to know what to look for—clues that warn of deterioration in hull and topside structure. He looks beyond the paint and putty that was applied the day before the ad was placed. Only a trained expert can determine the true condition—and value—of a used houseboat and save you a headache and money.

Should a naval architect or marine surveyor be unavailable, you may decide to proceed on your own.

Drydock Inspection for the Fiberglass Boat. Check the hull by looking for rough areas, especially below the waterline. Many patches may indicate considerable hull damage. Check for cracks and rotting, especially at points of stress: along the keel, in the area where the transom meets the hull, along the gunnels, the deck, cabin bulkheads, and on the inside of the hull. Check for soft spots by applying pressure with the hand. Check to see if deck canopies and roof decks are intended for topside use and will support walking or lounging. Changes in color values in the hull and superstructure may indicate age and deterioration. Be suspicious of fresh paint and new carpeting.

Metal-Hulled Boats. Check for extensive rust stains, especially on the back side of the rusted area, and with permission, apply the ice pick test; push firmly into the metal to ascertain what amount of rusting has occurred. The point will penetrate or puncture through rusted metal. A seller who objects to the ice pick test should be highly suspect.

Above the waterline check the cabin's juncture with the deckline, around fittings and cleats, and all welded seams. Check, too, along the keel and hull sides; bulges or dents that don't follow the normal hull lines indicate damage to the original structure.

Electrolysis damage (discussed earlier) inspection should include a search for pitting below the waterline, and if the hull is badly corroded, consider the cost of an overhaul by a qualified aluminum welder with special equipment.

The Inspection Afloat. Have the seller, or agent, pilot the craft at different speeds. While the vessel is underway, roam around and check the bilge area, where the bottom meets the water, for movement. Pulsating movements may be all right in a rough sea, but excessive hull throbbing may indicate faulty or broken stringers and framing that can lead to fatigue and ultimate breakdown. Check the lowest point in the hull for excessive water and traces of oil. Some water in the bilge is normal, but collecting water can indicate leaks from many sources.

Riding characteristics should be noted at slow, medium, and top speeds. Does the vessel shudder at top speed? Is there control at slow speeds? How is she on turns? Are there any annoying vibrations or noises from the engine or construction? Check the trim of the vessel underway and at rest for insights into design and equipment placement.

The engine should be checked by an experienced mechanic to ascertain its condition, and if work is needed, the probable cost of bringing the engine up to top performance. Is a major overhaul necessary? How long will it take? Is the shifting difficult? Oil dirty? The owner's manual, if the boat owner doesn't have it, can be obtained from the factory; study it for efficient operation and complete care.

Often when hull and engine repairs are necessary on a proposed purchase, and a cost estimate is made by a reputable repairman, the cost added to the selling price may still be within the range of a good buy. After all, all boat sellers are not trying to get rid of a lemon. The seller may be trading up to a bigger model, maybe the wife became disenchanted, or a young couple may have an addition to the family that requires the sale, or perhaps the owner is moving to the mountains. There are many legitimate reasons for putting up the "For Sale" sign on a houseboat.

DEFECT NOTIFICATION LAW

As with the automotive industry, consumer protection has entered the boating field. The U.S. Coast Guard issued its final 'rules on "Defect Notification," and they become operative on September 3, 1972. The defect notification regulation subjects the boatbuilders to the same rules now governing Detroit whereby autos with defects must be "recalled" for repair at no cost to the purchaser.

If the builder discovers a defect in his product or has some other fault that could involve safety or substantial risk of injury to the public, he must act within 30 days.

If the Coast Guard discovers a defect through testing, investigation, or examination of reports, it can require the manufacturer to issue an appropriate defect notification. The boat buyer, too, uncovering a defect, can first notify the manufacturer in writing with full details.

A copy of the letter should be sent to the Commandant (GBBC62), U.S. Coast Guard, 400 7th St., S.W., Washington, D.C. 20590. The boat buyer should attempt to resolve the defect with the manufacturer. If an impasse occurs, write the Commandant again.

Defect notifications must be sent out by the manufacturer to the first retail purchaser, the subsequent purchaser if known, the dealers or distributors, and the Commandant.

INSURANCE COVERAGE

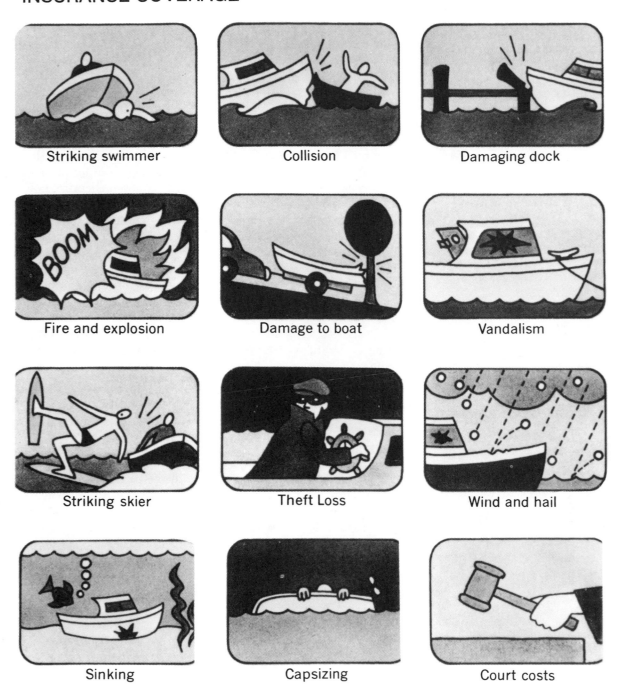

This graphic representation illustrates to the boat owner the items included in a complete-coverage insurance policy. (From: Allstate)

The many safety standards are too detailed to be discussed here. The complete information on regulations were published in the *Federal Register*, August 4, 1972. (Copies may be obtained, at 20 cents each, from the Superintendent of Documents, U.S. Government Printing Office, Washington, D.C. 20402.)

INSURANCE

Houseboat insurance gives protection against many hazards and accidents that stem from the complexity of increased boating participation. Policies are many and varied. The all-risk, or comprehensive, policy insures almost every occurrence, usually on a deductible basis, with the insured paying the first $50 or $100 of the claim. In addition to the houseboat, the outboard motor and trailer can also be separately insured.

Your policy should spell out the precise coverage offered and should include personal liability, property damage, and bodily injury. Insurance buys peace of mind, but expect to pay about 4 to 6 percent of the total value of an outboard-powered boat and a little more for the inboard boat. Rates are not rigidly established, and it is possible to wheel and deal with your agent to get the best package from various underwriters.

WARRANTY

Most houseboat companies guarantee their products for a certain period of time, usually for 1 year; that is, all the parts of the craft that they manufacture. Many components, such as engine, stove, head, appliances, and the like, are supplied by various companies, and each has its own guarantee. The houseboat, in effect, has many warranties. Study your warranty, know your guarantees, and follow all recommended procedures.

Uniflite touts their warranty, guaranteeing everything they have built, except the gel coat, for as long as the original purchaser owns the boat.

4

The Lexicon of
Houseboating

The lingo of sailors since the days of papyrus and balsa boats is a fascinating lore. The language is gingered up with salty terms and phrases that captain and crew use for quick and efficient communication. The unique vocabulary enables all aboard a houseboat to communicate intelligently in a dialogue that is essential to successful cruising.

TERMS RELATING TO THE CREW

Aboard   within, or on board the houseboat
Ahoy   nautical "hello" when hailing another vessel, or person
All hands   the entire crew
Aye   Yes, or I understand
Berth   the sleeping quarters of a person
Bowman   a crew member on the bow who may handle the anchor or
    serve as a lookout
Break out   the freeing of an anchor from the bottom
Chips   a nickname for the houseboat's carpenter
Corinthian   an amateur sailor
Coxswain   the person who steers the boat and has charge of her
Crew   the people aboard who help run a boat
Davy Jones   the spirit of the sea
Davy Jones Locker   the bottom of the sea
Hail   speaking or calling to another boat or to crew in another part of
    the boat

Hand   one of the crew to assist as in "lend a hand" or hurry as in "bear a hand"

Helmsman   one who steers the boat

Land ho   the cry used for spotting land when coming in from a wide expanse of water

Log book   a journal kept by the skipper in which wind, weather, distances, and all important news is noted

Lubber   a greenhorn aboard a boat; a land lubber

Master   see "skipper"

Mate   an officer ranking next to the master, in houseboating usually the wife, who also can be called the Cruise Director

Owner's flag   the private flag of a boat owner, often self-designed

Port Captain   the official in charge of harbor activity

Quarters   accommodations and living areas aboard a boat

Skipper   the master or captain of a houseboat

Spell   to spell is to relieve another of any work

Stand by   to be prepared to act immediately

Stevedore   a person who loads or unloads cargo

Stow   to pack the cargo

Trick   a person's allotted time at the helm, as a trick at the wheel

Watch   a division of time on board ship during which crew members are on lookout duty

NAUTICAL TERMS RELATING TO THE HOUSEBOAT

Knowledge of the following terminology will help you to become houseboat oriented. This basic lexicon will be of import to fuller enjoyment through salty conversation about the houseboat, its description, characteristics, and accessories.

Abaft   the stern (rear) area

Abeam   at right angles to the keel of a houseboat; referring to an object or condition outside the boat

Above   upstairs, as on deck, or on top of the cabin (sun deck)

Afore   toward the bow (front) of a houseboat

Aft   toward the stern, or behind the boat, depending upon where the speaker is standing

Aloft   above deck, or overhead

Amidships   in or toward the middle of a houseboat, halfway between the bow and stern

Anchor   a shaped and weighted device of iron or steel used to hold a boat in position when dropped to the bottom; also called a "hook"

Beam   width of the houseboat at its widest part

Below   downstairs, under the deck

B.I.A.   Boating Industry Association, a marine trade group and information center headquartered at 333 N. Michigan Ave., Chicago, Ill. 60601

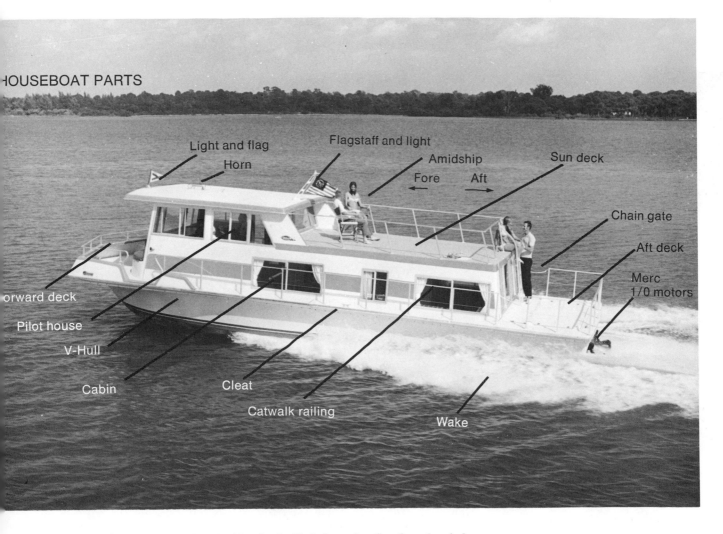

Light and flag
Horn
Flagstaff and light
Amidship
Fore   Aft
Sun deck
Chain gate
Aft deck
Merc 1/0 motors
orward deck
Pilot house
V-Hull
Cabin
Cleat
Catwalk railing
Wake

Bilge   the lowest section inside the hull, below the floorboards of the cabin

Boat hook   a long staff with an attached iron hook used to pick up a mooring line or to hold on to a dock or other boat

Bow   forward part of the houseboat

Bow line   a mooring or dock line led forward through the bow chock

Broadside   the whole side (port or starboard) of a houseboat

Bunk   bed on board the boat

Cabin   the living quarters aboard a houseboat

Catamaran   a boat hull type consisting of two hulls held together by a wing deck that supports the superstructure

Caulking   oakum or cotton used to fill the seams of a boat to make it watertight

Chine   lower edge of the hull where the sides and bottom join

Chock   a fitting through which the mooring and anchoring line are run

Cleat   metal or wood T-shaped fitting for securing lines

Companionway   stairway from deck to cabin or space below

Cradle   a frame that supports a boat when out of water

Davit   timber, piping, or iron cranes projecting over the houseboat's side, or stern, for hoisting or carrying small boats

Davits properly secure a dinghy and through the use of gunwale clamps are capable of holding fast the auxiliary boat in rough seas. (Bremen Mfg. Co.)

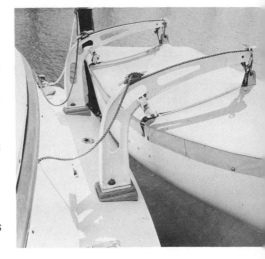

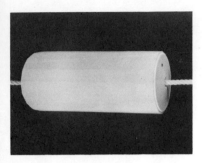

One type of fender can be used horizontally or vertically in singles or in series of two or more; it is unaffected by gasoline, oil, or salt water. (N. A. Taylor Co.)

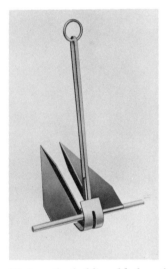

Flukes, the holding blades of an anchor, dig into the river's bottom. (N. A. Taylor Co.)

Deck   the floor/s of a houseboat

Dinghy   a small open boat used as an auxiliary for a houseboat

Displacement   the weight of water displaced by a boat

Draft   the depth of water required to float a houseboat

Drag   the hull's resistance to movement caused by the water's friction

Dry rot   soft and spongy wood infected by a fungus that thrives in moist, dark, unventilated places

Even keel   the position of a houseboat, well balanced, sitting evenly and level in the water, in proper trim

Fenders   air cushions, stuffed bags, rope, or wood hung over the side of a houseboat to protect it from chafing

Fiberglass   woven, matted, or powdered glass cloth bonded together with a resin adhesive to produce a strong houseboat material

Fitting out   preparing the boat at the start of the season, or after a lengthy lay-up period

Flotation   specialized structure and materials built into the hull of the houseboat to prevent it from sinking when punctured or swamped

Flukes   the blades of an anchor that dig into the sand or mud to hold the boat in place

Fore   forward part of a houseboat, things forward of amidships

Forward   up front

Freeboard   distance from waterline to the top of hull

Galley   kitchen

Gunwale (gunnel)   the upper rail, top edge of a hull

Hatch   an opening in the deck to afford a passage up and down

Hawser   a large, heavy line used for various purposes

Head   the toilet compartment

Helm   wheel or tiller that controls the direction of a houseboat underway

Hold   interior of a houseboat where cargo is stored

Hook   anchor

Hull   hollow body or shell, the lowest part of a boat

Galley with propane stove and wet bar (Kayot)

Berth converts from a dinette. (Burns Craft)

Inboard-outboard engine   separate power and propulsion units hooked to form a drive package

Keel   strip of wood or metal on the underside of the hull that runs along the center of the bottom; sometimes, two or more keels are used

Lash   to tie, make secure, with a line

Lay-up   to take a houseboat out of water, as at the end of the season or for repairs

Line   twisted cord of various diameters, rarely called rope aboard ship

L.O.A.   length overall

Locker   a box or chest used for storing things

Main deck   usually the principal, or highest deck of a boat

Marina   a boat basin serving houseboats in launching, mooring, provisioning, repair, and so on

Painter   a line attached to the bow, used for making her fast

Planking   the thick strong boards that cover the sides and deck of boat

Port   the left side of a houseboat as you face forward

Rode   the anchor line

Sheathing   the protective casing or covering of a boat's bottom or hull

Shipshape   clean and orderly condition

Ship water   to take in water over the gunwale, or side, as in a heavy sea

Starboard   the right side of the houseboat when facing forward

Stern   the aft section, or rear of the hull or deck

Stringer   longitudinal member inside the hull sides that ties the ribs together

Stow   to put away gear or cargo

Swab   a mop used to clean up, wash down, or dry a deck

Topsides   on deck, that part of the hull above water

Trim   to adjust cargo to proper angle or draft

Transom   the back of the boat, across the stern

V-hull   a modified hull which is V-shape forward and tapers to a flat, or planing, bottom at the stern

Waterline   line where the surface of the water touches the hull when the houseboat is anchored

The marina supplies water, electricity.

Helmsman's instrument panel and wheel (Aqua-meter)

Wheel   steering wheel connected mechanically to a rudder or propellers for steering control

Yaw   to swing back and forth without control, as a boat in a heavy sea or while being towed

THE LANGUAGE OF NAVIGATION

Listed are the more common terms dealing with houseboat navigation. Clear and simple definitions, which can be quickly learned, are noted. Only through constant use will the definitions become "second nature." While underway, the dialogue between captain and crew must be adequate to communicate observations, sounds, and conditions outside and aboard the houseboat.

Bell buoy

Can buoy

Abreast   alongside of, as when two boats are side by side

Afloat   to be buoyed up by water

Aground   condition of boat's hull touching bottom

Ahead   the direction toward which the boat points

Alongsides   beside another boat or dock

Beacon   warning device placed over shoal, bank, or rock to call attention to it

Bearing   direction of an object in relation to the boat

Bear off   steer away from, to avoid

Bell buoy   a floating device with a warning bell, placed to mark the limits of a channel

Bight   bend in a shoreline; also the bend of a rope when it is folded

Binnacle   protective housing for the compass

Blow   describing a strong wind or storm

Buoy   a moored float or marker to mark a channel

Buoyage   system of buoys placed to indicate channels and make navigation safer and easier

Burdened   a boat not having the right of way

Can buoy   black buoy with an odd number, placed on the port side of a channel or river as you enter

Cast off   to release the lines from a dock of mooring in preparation for getting underway

Channel   a deep section of water through shallow depths, marked with buoys for safe passage

Chart   a marine map, usually denoting depths of water, channels, buoys, navigational aids, and hazards

Chop   short, sharp, irregular waves caused by the action of wind or tide

Compass   instrument with magnetized needle which tends to point to the magnetic north, used aboard a boat to aid in directing the boat on course

Course   a plotted and planned direction of route

Dead ahead   directly in front of the houseboat

Dead astern   directly behind

Degree   1-36oth of a circle

Depth finder electronic device that bounces sound waves off the water's bottom and records the depth; also used to locate fish

Eddy roily water caused by the meeting of opposite currents

Fairway an open, navigable water course

Fathom unit of measure equaling 6 feet

Fend to push away

Flotsam floating debris

Following seas waves coming from the stern of a boat

Hard over the most extreme change in a boat's course, caused by turning the wheel as far as possible to one side or the other

Headway forward movement of a houseboat

Heave to point the boat into the wind, without concern for headway, as in riding out a heavy sea

Knot a nautical unit of speed (not distance)

Land mark navigational mark, or reference on land

Latitude degree of distance north and south of the equator

Lee sheltered from the wind

Lee shore sheltered shore, out of the wind

Leeward direction away from the wind

Life buoy ring-shaped flotation collar for emergency use

List inclination of a boat to one side when the load is unbalanced

Longitude degree of distance east and west of a given point on charts

Lying to holding the boat in a stationary position

Make fast secure the boat line to a cleat or other tie

Mooring place where a houseboat is made fast by anchor, or tied alongside a dock or float

Nun buoy a red buoy with a conical top

The depth finder is rapidly becoming a standard piece of equipment for boats of all sizes.

Nun buoy

A recessed model compass features precise positioning and shape to provide best magnification for clarity at extreme viewing angles. (Aqua Meter Instrument Co.)

Privileged   the boat that has the right of way

Shoal   shallow area in the water

Sound   to probe and determine the depth of water

Steady   to keep the wheel (helm) position as is

Surf   breaking of waves upon the shore

Swamp   to sink by filling with water

Trim   the condition of a boat, angle and draft, with reference to her cargo and ballast

True North   the geographic North Pole through which all meridians pass

Trough   the hollow between crests of waves

Variation   compass degree variation between magnetic north and true north

Wake   the V-trail of waves a boat leaves behind her when underway

Weigh anchor   to hoist the anchor in preparation to getting underway

5

Afloat and Underway

If you're concerned about your inexperience and ability to handle a houseboat, remember that you don't have to know it all—no one knows it all. If you live to be a hundred, you'll never encompass the dimensions of boating. The tricky art of plying the water is as old as mankind, yet as new as the stern drive. Rental marinas entrust their expensive houseboats to inexperienced landlubbers, retirees cruise extensively along coastal, Great Lakes, and river routes, and statistically, the "first time" skipper seldom racks up a boat, or gets into serious trouble. All of which should put your mind at ease when for the first time you take to sea.

Your baptism with a new or unfamiliar houseboat should be on calm waters under ideal weather conditions. Experience at the helm teaches: how much room the boat needs to turn a complete circle; the distance it takes to slow down from high speed to low, to stop; the responses to the turn of the helm; the boat's reaction to sudden gusts of wind or wake from other boats. All boats, except the double-ended canoe, in plowing through the water produce a wake, and the surge of water can be disruptive to the shoreline through erosion, or to other boats in many ways, banging them against each other or against docks, causing anything from a spilled cup of hot coffee to swamping or capsizing a small boat. Five miles an hour is a safe speed.

Experiencing the feeling of the houseboat under differing situations and conditions is how experience and know-how are gained. There is no set curriculum, course of study, or graduation that denotes a competent seaman; it's largely a matter of spending hours at the helm and

Vision of 360 degrees is possible from the flying bridge of this Merc-powered houseboat.

experiencing the craft in relation to varying water conditions. If your baptism is difficult, remember that in adversity we learn.

Progressively, you tackle more difficult situations: controlling the houseboat in rough seas, quartering the turbulence of wakes at approximately 45 degrees; running the dangerous course before huge waves when the boat is lifted by the stern, bringing the rudder and propeller up clear of the water. Control gone, the boat can turn broadside in the trough (called broaching) and become vulnerable to the waves spilling over the gunwales. Broaching is prevented by some semblance of control, best achieved by throttling down and heading into the waves at a slight angle so that the power gives steerage and control but not necessarily forward progress.

A houseboat steers from the stern, and to turn, it is necessary to leave adequate room for the stern to clear obstacles. Also, remember that the houseboat sideslips on turns. And the heavier the boat the more difficult it is to stop; therefore, use short bursts of power in reverse. The houseboat is not made for speed, and its most comfortable and efficient speed is not wide open. Driving the engine full speed for extended periods of time will greatly increase the fuel bill and also reduce the comfort factor for all aboard. The moderate speed of a houseboat (4 to 14 miles an hour) enables travel of 60 to 100 miles a day, and offers cruising safety and scenery enjoyment that are lost at higher speeds.

The experienced pilot runs his houseboat at full power to a level planing position on the water, and then throttles back to a comfortable cruising speed, yet maintaining the planing position. Running too slow can also be inefficient. A high-riding bow, low stern, and large wake indicate a drag on the engine and call for throttling up or down until proper balance is achieved.

The skipper should have good steering vision astern and abeam, as well as ahead. The large model houseboats have a control station on the top deck (flying bridge) which provides 360-degree vision. It is only under ideal conditions that the piloting of a houseboat is as simple as driving a car—a claim made by some manufacturers. The surroundings of the houseboat—broad expanses of water, strong winds, tide and current conditions, fuel limitations—all tie in with the boat's limitations of design, range, and control to engender a respect for its limitations. Respect must also be accorded to the forces of nature. Wind and water, in times of nature tantrums, can produce more powerful forces than any ever generated by man. The houseboat's design can make it difficult to maneuver and control in adverse wind-water conditions because, for one, they greatly affect the steering efficiency, and outrunning them may be difficult.

THE LANGUAGE OF CHARTS

The chart (never call it a map) is akin to the roadmap of the land-lubber motorist; it shows distances, directions, and speed limits, but beyond that, the chart is more complex, precise, informative, and expensive.

The houseboater uses the chart for his intended area of participation—coastal waterway, Great Lakes, or rivers—and a study of it gives an excellent picture of the water and land characteristics. He learns water depths and the characteristics of the bottom; the features of the banks or shoreline; where the harbors and ports can be found; landmarks, man-made and natural; numbered and colored buoys and other aids to navigation. The skipper, on a compass course, checks the chart against his speed and what he observes, and the true position of the houseboat may be estimated most of the way.

Compass readings by the skipper must take into account the variation between "true" and "magnetic" north before a cruise. This is especially important when the cruise is extensive, and may traverse areas with geographical variations.

Measuring Time and Distance. Charts are used to estimate the expected duration of a trip, the distance already traveled at any point in the voyage, and the actual speed of the houseboat. A stop watch and a fairly reliable speedometer are needed. The method to predict the time a trip will consume is to add up the miles (measured from the chart) and divide by the average speed that the boat maintains. As an example, if a trip logs 40 miles, and the boat cruises at 10 miles an hour, the trip will consume 4 hours. Such a computation is too ideal, as it does not allow for many factors that will affect the run. Compensations for these effects will make an estimate more valid.

Measurement of Depth is of principal concern to skippers. The depths listed on charts for coastal waters are at low tide, and on inland lakes and rivers low-water levels are indicated. Notes on the margins of charts tell the tide range. This information is of great value to the houseboater, as a high-tide figure will be greater than the depth recorded on the chart, which is at low tide, and allows a wider range of cruising, permitting passage through certain inlets and other shallow areas. Charts include extensive information on the water's depth so that a glance will give the skipper a good reference to the water's bottom. Only the more significant and representative depths are noted, and when the figures are widely spaced, the skipper can be assured of a reasonably flat or uniformly sloping bottom. Near the shore dotted lines called depth curves appear connecting points of equal depth.

Bottom Features are indicated on the charts and include such information as "hard": rock, sand, coral, and the like, or "soft": mud, grass, and so forth.

Land Mass Features. Details of land characteristics, near the shoreline and of such a prominent nature as to be seen clearly, serve as aids to navigation, and are faithfully noted on nautical charts. The topography is indicated by contour lines, heights in elevation, terrain formations, locations of steep slopes, and the type of vegetation. All are indicated by symbols or wording where such information may be of use to the skipper.

Man-made Land Features. Nautical charts also note man-made features on land. Certain types of landmarks are more often used by skippers, and are indicated as building or house, chimney, flagpole, spire, dome, cupola, radio tower, antenna, tanks of various types, and conspicuous trees.

Standardized symbols and abbreviations are necessary to cram a vast amount of information on a chart, as many items must be concentrated in a small area. All charts carry a table which explains symbols and abbreviations, and also a table for the conversion of meters, fathoms, and feet. An up-to-date chart is replete with information that should put the skipper's mind at ease. You cruise on water marked by various buoys and markers, and by checking the various landmarks en route, you have a continuous and valid reference.

On extended trips, especially on unknown waters, it is necessary to have charts of the area. A little time spent poring over the charts will give many insights into the nature of the waters: landmarks and aids to navigation, general topography, information for selecting an anchorage for the night or for a haven in bad weather.

Charts are printed on heavy paper by various agencies of the government to furnish the boater up-to-date, revised, and accurate information on navigable waters.

Charts for coastal waters of the United States, including harbors, and rivers extending inland to the head of tidal action, are issued by: U.S. Coast and Geodetic Survey, ESSA, Rockville, Maryland 20852. Their chart catalog is issued in three volumes: 1 covers the U.S. Atlantic and Gulf coastal waters; 2 covers the West Coast and Pacific Islands; and 3 covers the Alaska Coast.

Charts of the high seas and foreign waters, a must for the houseboater intent on cruising the Caribbean, are issued by: U.S. Naval Oceanographic Office, Washington, D.C. 20390. The chart catalog is issued by regions at 25¢ each. Region "O" covers United States Coastal Waters. Region "2" covers the Bahamian and West Indian cruising areas and the waters bordering Central and South America.

Charts of the Great Lakes and major inland rivers, like the Mississippi and the Ohio, as well as a chart catalog of Lake Champlain, the New York Barge Canal System, and other waters are issued by: U.S. Army Engineer District, Lake Survey, 630 Federal Bldg., Detroit, Michigan 48226.

Charts can be purchased from the above agencies, or their field offices, or from retail sales agents that abound in areas of extensive boating activity.

NAVIGATION KNOW-HOW

An unofficial definition of navigation can be explained as know-how in conducting a houseboat along a watercourse where landmarks and various types of navigation aids are used, for fixing one's position, and making possible the following of a safe course.

The houseboater seldom travels beyond the sight of land, and his waterway is mostly well-marked and is more often shallow than deep, more often windless than stormy. Extensive navigational knowledge is always desirable but, for the houseboater, not absolutely necessary. The navigation techniques used by most houseboat skippers plying favored and protected waters consist of chart orientation, observation of buoys and landmarks, and the use of other aids to navigation. Position, for the most part, is by continuous visual reference to the reliable buoys and markers; the Coast Guard expends much effort in keeping them valid. While proceeding down most rivers and channels, you'll find positioning informal and plotting quite unnecessary. Navigational information for the houseboater can best be obtained from the most simple and logical of visual bearings, those directly ahead or broad on the beam. Taking bearings dead ahead can be accomplished by the helmsman alone.

The deepest part of a narrow watercourse may be expected in its center along straight stretches and at the outside of curves. To keep a straight course learn to select a distant point, and with a little wheel turning in either direction, you'll progress with a minimum of zigzagging. The early morning mists, common to river travel, may affect the sighting of buoys, while references to imposing landmarks on the shore may be more pronounced. Use them for confirmation of your route. In all situations where there is an absence of surface aids, the skipper should refer to the chart for natural landmarks on shore.

In tight corners, or on sharp curves of narrow waterways, throttle down and sound a long warning blast. Learn to know the story behind ripples, eddies, white caps, and differing water colors, along with the clues contained in wind shifts, gathering clouds, and lowering temperature. Knowing exactly where you are most of the time is a must on the open sea. Orientation on big water requires of the skipper the use of many position-determining instruments and such techniques as "line of position," plotting a true bearing with a pelorus, plotting horizontal angles with a three-arm protractor, and using the sextant, optical range finder, and many other aids. The mastery and use of these instruments are rarely within the experiential background of most houseboat skippers.

A veteran Great Lakes and Caribbean captain (not a houseboater), when asked about a navigation problem, exclaimed, "Hell, if you're in trouble just grab the bow line, go over the side, wade to shore, and pull the boat after you." Though an oversimplification, the advice can put the mind at ease for the skipper who feels that the intricacies of navigation are too much.

THE BUOYAGE SYSTEM

The unique system of buoys aids navigation by the placement of markers and guides on navigable waters to indicate shallow waters, channels, obstructions, hidden dangers, and other information. The United States Coast Guard is the agency responsible for the placement and maintenance of these aids to navigation, which enable the boater to follow natural and improved channels, and to provide a continuous reference for coast, river, and lake piloting.

Objects that have been primarily established as aids to navigation include: buoys, beacons, major lighthouses with radio beacons, fog signals, and an array of visible, audible, and electronic systems.

The shape and color of a buoy conveys to the skipper information as to his location, the best travel route, and the limits of a safe course. Buoys may be lighted or unlighted, audible or visible, or a combination of several. Buoys are the mariner's road signs, and they are distinguished by shape, number, color, and signaling characteristic.

When your boat enters a harbor from seaward, buoys marking the channel's port side are black and odd-numbered. The numbers on the buoys start from seaward and progress, numerically, up the channel. Remembering the 3 R's helps to fix these principles in mind: "Red, Right, Returning"—indicating red colored buoy, on the starboard side, when returning from seaward. Obviously, in going out to sea, the reverse is the case. Likewise, "Bore" gives a reminder on the numbering system: Black *o*dd, *r*ed *e*ven.

Buoys of other colors are used, but not often encountered by houseboats. As to buoy shapes, the nun buoy, painted red, is a cylinder of steel with a cone-shaped top. The can buoy, painted black, is a cylinder of steel with straight sides, and flat top.

Although the Coast Guard anchors buoys with concrete blocks, ranging from 1 to 5 tons, their position may not be an absolute indication of what they purport to point out. Bad storms, heavy tides, collision by boats, and other accidents have been known to sink and move buoys far from their original placement. Also, many times fisher-

Buoys, Waterway Markers

These are your water highway sign posts. Learn them, learn what they mean.

When entering a harbor keep the red buoys on your right and the black ones on your left. The red buoys will be even-numbered and the black odd-numbered. This is summed up in the words, "red right returning."

"Returning", in this case, means entering the harbor from seaward. When a harbor has two entrances "entering" means coming in from the north or east.

Federal Waterway Markers

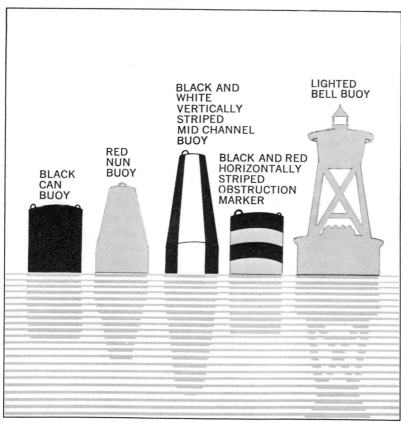

Buoys, waterway markers, intercoastal beacons (From: Mobil Safety Afloat)

Intracoastal Beacons

On The Intracoastal Waterway, the buoyage system is somewhat different, and the markers may be on land.

Uniform State Waterway Marking System

This is a system of marking the waterways located entirely within the boundaries of a state, such as lakes or rivers. The navigation signals are similar to the Federal ones (red and black buoys in pairs). The "Regulatory Markers" may be signs or painted buoys, international orange on a white background.

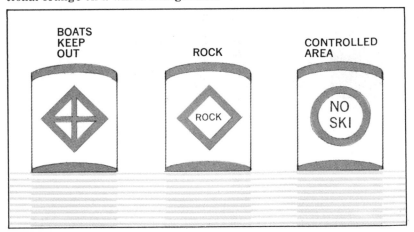

Buoys, waterway markers, intercoastal beacons (From: Mobil Safety Afloat)

men in boats will cluster around a buoy and conceal it from a cruising boat. If the chart indicates its presence, search for the screened-out marker.

Lights. Lighted buoys are used to mark turning points in a channel or river, underwater obstructions, and the middle safe area. Lighted buoys vary in both color and characteristic of their light: starboard side, entering from seaward, the color will be white or red; port side, entering from seaward, the color will be white or green. These channel lights may be flashing, occulting, or quick flashing—marking a spot requiring special caution.

Other Aids to Navigation. Sound buoys are equipped with a characteristic sound to aid in their location during such periods of reduced visibility as darkness, heavy rain, and fog. The bell buoy carries a bell that gongs from the motion of sea. Where wave action is insufficient, bell buoys are operated by batteries. The gong buoy substitutes a set of four gongs for the bell, and tappers strike against the gongs to sound four different notes in an irregular sequence. The whistle buoy provides an audible signal for the boater; it is sounded by compressed air that is produced by the motion of the buoy in a ground swell. The spar buoy is a long tapered log or steel column used primarily for day marks in lightly trafficked channels. Day beacons are unlighted fixed structures, normally equipped with a pointer, signboard, or day marks.

The foregoing indicates that sight and sound in buoyage are combined to enable the houseboater to find his way safely in unknown waters and in adverse weather conditions. A skipper should know the language of buoys and understand what he sees and hears. Beyond that, he should get a copy of the United States Coast Pilot for the area of interest. The publication includes charts, light lists, detailed information about the coast line, port information, weather, radio service, fuel sources, and services available.

Write: Department of Commerce, Coast and Geodetic Survey, Washington, D.C. (Indicate section of coast desired; price: $1.)

WIND WARNING SIGNALS

That old nautical truism, "Red sky at morning, sailors take warning," maintains its integrity to the experienced salt, and equally to the weekend boater—if he's smart. The validity of the slogan can be seen on any federal, state, or local township flagpole near the water when the weather makes news. The red can either be found on one pennant, two pennants, a square flag with a black square center, or two flags of the same design, but they all signify one thought for the houseboater— weather warning!

One red pennant tells the houseboater that small craft warnings are up and cautions against venturing far from shore, if your houseboat is not equipped to handle rough waters, persistent winds up to 38 miles an hour and possible rain. At night, one red light above one white light means houseboat warnings.

Warning Display Signals

SMALL CRAFT*

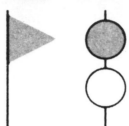

DAYTIME: Red Pennant.

NIGHTTIME: Red Light Over White Light.

Indicates: Forecast winds as high as 33 knots and sea conditions considered dangerous to small-craft operations.

GALE

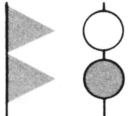

DAYTIME: Two Red Pennants.

NIGHTTIME: White Light Over Red Light.

Indicates: Forecast winds in the range 34-47 knots.

STORM

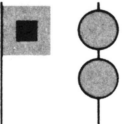

DAYTIME: Square Red Flag With Black Square Centered.

NIGHTTIME: Two Red Lights.

Indicates: Forecast winds 48 knots and above no matter how high the wind speed. If the winds are associated with a tropical cyclone (hurricane), storm warnings indicate forecast winds of 48-63 knots.

HURRICANE

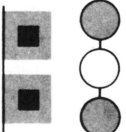

DAYTIME: Two Square Red Flags With Black Squares Centered.

NIGHTTIME: White Light Between Two Red Lights.

Indicates: Forecast winds of 64 knots and above, displayed only in connection with a hurricane.

Two red pennants signify gale force winds and heavy seas, which for coastal boaters means trouble and that it would be best to remain ashore. Gale force winds can reach up to 54 miles an hour, and seas up to 10 feet. No fun to be cruising in, no matter what size the houseboat.

Storm warnings are given by a single square flag with a black square center. Winds are rated at 55 miles an hour, and above. Seas are extremely heavy, so stay in port. The night signal for this prediction would be two red lights.

Hurricane winds are denoted by two red flags with black squares by day and at night by a single white light between two red lights. Winds reach upward of 70 miles an hour, with tremendous seas. Forget houseboating, batten down the hatches, secure the craft, and wait it out.

Other types of weather warning assistance are given by local newspapers, television and radio stations, and the nearest marina. If your houseboat is equipped with a marine radio, your nearest Coast Guard station broadcasts weather announcements. There are also Coastal Warning Facilities Charts for the serious-minded houseboater. The charts can be obtained by writing the National Weather Service, Washington, D.C. Always be sure about weather conditions before you leave port. If the sky looks threatening, don't go out. The weather always clears up; it's just a matter of waiting. However, if you're out and do get caught in a bad storm, keep the bow headed at an angle into the waves, don't try to cross a large body of water, and keep as close to the shore as safely possible.

6

Nautical Rules
of the Road

Rules of conduct afloat represent carefully considered regulations, and the duties and actions of the skipper in practically every situation that is encountered on water are definitely prescribed. The Inland Rules of the Road, enacted by the Congress of the United States, are law, as are the International Rules of the Road, adapted by many maritime nations. Both sets of rules include a wide range of subjects concerned with the proper handling of boats: avoidance of collision, rights of way, whistle signals, lighting standards, fog signals, essential equipment, adequate piloting equipment, knowledge of buoyage systems, currents and tides, and many other lesser allied subjects.

An insight into some of the most important Rules of the Road is here noted: The fundamental purpose of the Rules of the Road is to prevent collision. The failure of a vessel to take special precautions during the constant-bearing approach of an oncoming vessel may constitute negligence. When there is present a risk of collision, both vessels are required to slow, or stop, or reverse, whichever is the safest course.

In preventing collision between two vessels, one of the two must necessarily be considered to have the right of way. This vessel is called "privileged." The other, which is the vessel that must give way, is called "burdened."

Sailboats, canoes, rowboats, and other unpowered craft almost always have the right of way (privileged) over powerboats. The only exception is when the unpowered craft is overtaking, or passing, a motorboat.

When overtaking and passing another boat, the boat being overtaken is privileged and has the right of way. In such a case the privilege rests with the leading boat; the overtaking boat is burdened, and has the duty not to pass until it can be safely done.

The area around a boat, clockwise from dead ahead to two points abaft the starboard beam, is called the "danger zone." This area represents the skipper's greatest concern because any other boats located in this danger zone, approaching the course of his boat, have the right of way. The responsibility lies in keeping clear of boats in the danger zone. However, boats located outside of your danger zone, and approaching your course, must give way to you.

When approaching another boat at right angles or obliquely, the boat on the right (starboard side) is privileged and has the right of way. The skippers exchange one short blast of the whistle; usually the privileged vessel should blow first, but either may.

In case of accident between vessels, it is the duty of the skipper of each vessel to stand by, ascertain assistance needed, and render such help as may be practicable and necessary to crew, skipper, and passengers. The name of the vessel and her home port must be given when requested, and serious accidents must be reported to the Coast Guard.

When two vessels are approaching each other head on, or nearly so, swing to the starboard, and thus pass port side to port side. This is preceded by a short one-blast whistle signal.

When two vessels are approaching each other, and either fails to understand the signals, course, or intention of the other for any reason, the vessel in doubt should immediately give the danger signal of four or more short blasts of the whistle.

When a vessel is coming out of a slip or mooring, dock or pier, passing signals do not apply until she is entirely clear. Upon leaving her pier or slip, the boat must sound one long blast; then, when she is clear of obstruction, the regular passing signals and rights of way apply.

The Rules of the Road include regulations concerning many other items:

BURDENED VESSEL

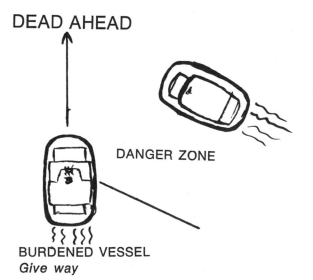

DEAD AHEAD

PRIVILEGED VESSEL
Hold course and speed

DANGER ZONE

BURDENED VESSEL
Give way

Boats on opposite parallel courses

Boats on parallel courses heading in the same direction

Method of giving whistle, bell, and horn signals

Rights of tow boats

Rights of way of ferry boats

Differences between International, Inland, and Great Lakes rules

RULES DIFFER BY REGIONS

Although there is a consistency in all Rules of the Road—International, Inland, Great Lakes, and Western River—there's also some regional variance dealing with situations afloat.

A houseboat cruising a combination of ocean and inland waters may well find herself under the jurisdiction of differing sets of rules. International Rules in a given situation may require one signal, Inland Rules another, and Great Lakes and Western River Rules may completely ignore the situation. On the other hand, rules to cover a given situation may be entirely different in each of the four jurisdictions. Yet, the individual characteristics of the four regions must be understood, because the Rules of the Road are mandatory for all vessels, and they must be properly obeyed.

The Coast Guard, as well as local marine police, aren't going to accept ignorance of the law as an excuse for improper boat operating procedure. The Rules of the Road are available to all, and houseboaters had better have them well committed to memory before leaving the dock.

Coast Guard publications, available free, give the full text of rules and regulations and should be in the pilothouse of every houseboat. Order by section:

International-Inland Rules of the Road CG-169

Great Lakes Rules of the Road CG-172

Western Rivers Rules of the Road CG-184

Copies are available from your nearest Marine Inspection Office of the Coast Guard, or write: Commandant (CHS), U.S. Coast Guard Headquarters, Washington, D.C. 20226.

FEDERAL BOAT SAFETY ACT

The boating business is booming with approximately 50 million participants in 1972, according to the Boating Industry Association, and the figure keeps increasing each year, indicating a very broad base of people. Unfortunately, that broad spectrum of humans includes the irresponsible and undisciplined who disregard all Rules of the Road and who have little respect for the rights of others. This group, which gives the majority a bad image, is going to find regulations a lot tougher, but in the long run they too will agree with the benefits.

The Federal Boat Safety Act of 1971 is aimed both at the owner and the houseboat manufacturer. The owner is subject to regulations concerning use of the boat, rendering aid in emergencies, safety standards, and penalties for operating his craft in a negligent manner. The manufacturer is held to a given set of standards of performance—criteria for what his vessel and certain of its equipment must do—and much more.

To cut through the legal jargon and technical phrasing of the Federal Boat Safety Act (Public Law 92-75), the Boating Industry Association, which has worked closely with the Department of Transportation and Coast Guard officials in the writing of the act, has simplified the language and analyzed the act for the layman.

Rather than a complete analysis of the act, those sections that relate to the houseboat owner, renter, operator, or passenger are indicated here in brief:

SECTION 5 empowers the Coast Guard to require certain equipment for safety reasons, to establish minimum safety standards for boats and associated equipment, and to determine if safety standards are being met by manufacturers.

SECTION 6 indicates guidelines and limitation upon the Coast Guard to assure responsible, reasonable, and workable standards and regulations.

SECTION 7 authorizes the Coast Guard to establish and check all equipment standards.

SECTION 10 establishes exclusive federal jurisdiction over manufacturing standards.

SECTION 12 defines "Prohibited Acts" as things the manufacturer and the owner/operator cannot do. Those related to the manufacturer are designed to protect the customer. Subsections are aimed at the owner/operator, and include such items as following the Rules of the Road, being considerate of others, and using the houseboat sensibly.

SECTION 15 requires manufacturers to inform customers when a defect of construction or design is discovered in their product. If you buy the houseboat "used" send to the manufacturer of the boat a registered letter identifying the model by number, listing serial numbers, and telling from whom you purchased it. Then you are treated by the manufacturer as the original owner.

SECTION 16 relates to the obligation to render assistance to casualties and aid to a vessel in trouble, so long as it does not endanger your own safety or craft. Subsection B protects those rendering aid from legal action for civil damages so long as reasonably prudent acts are performed in giving such assistance.

SECTION 22 relates to the issuance of safety certificates by the various states, which in effect will probably lead to the licensing of boat users.

SECTION 33 establishes a Boating Safety Advisory Council to be comprised of 21 representatives of the public, federal and state agencies, boating associations, and manufacturers. The group is to advise the Coast Guard on boating safety matters and on carrying out its responsibilities under the act. Thus the public, industry, and the Coast Guard are involved in the safety program.

SECTION 35 relates to the penalties for noncompliance by manufacturers at $2,000 per violation.

SECTION 37 requires the Coast Guard to establish an accident reporting system in order to amass data, the results of which can aid craft designers and manufacturers to make safer and bugproof craft and equipment. The owner/operator is required to report any accident in which his craft is involved, in the manner required by the agency having jurisdiction over the waterway on which the accident occurred.

The other sections of the act do not cover anything the houseboater can or must do. In summary, then, the first direct benefit to the houseboater is the provision which establishes standards for construction and equipment, based on meeting performance criteria. Another benefit to the customer is the requirement that manufacturers must keep records to certify that all standards are complied with on every vessel built and sold. A plate, stating the manufacturer's compliance, is to be attached to every vessel leaving the production line.

Another benefit of the act is that the continuing program of research and development by manufacturers, associations, individuals, and government is bound to result in ever-improving products and better buys for the customer.

THE WASTE-DISCHARGE DILEMMA

All boats that have live-aboard potential are in a temporary dilemma because of the 1970 regulations preventing waste discharge into navigable waters. A human being gives off considerable waste products in the course of a day. In the past, these human, and other, wastes were dumped directly into the waters or they were stored in a holding tank, then after 40 toilet flushes, more or less, were emptied at a pump-out station. New York and others have a holding tank law on the books, but it is impossible for boats to comply, as the pump-out facilities are inadequate. Among the nation's boatmen, there's an overwhelming opinion against the compulsory use of holding tanks. In fact, to this day, no satisfactory method of waste discharge has been developed, and to prevent further deterioration of our nation's waters, a law was enacted.

PUBLIC LAW 91-224, The Water Quality Improvement Act of 1970, contains provisions for the purpose of preventing the discharge of untreated, or inadequately treated, sewage into the navigable waters of the United States.

The law will be implemented by promulgation of standards and regulations, by certification of waste disposal devices, by research and study, and by enforcement. The standards were drawn up by the Environmental Protection Agency (EPA) in cooperation with the Coast Guard, the Departments of the Navy and the Interior, the Army Corps of Engineers, and the National Science Foundation.

One or several sewage treatment systems may eventually become satisfactory in fulfilling the requirements of the law and give the boat owner a choice of systems. Already, many companies are working on devices utilizing various principles: The macerator-chlorinator, unacceptable at present, may evolve into an effective certifiable system of treating raw sewage. Another device operates on the principle of destructive distillation. The system is connected to toilet and bath facilities and includes a mixing tank, telemetering device, and reactor. The solid waste is broken down into liquid, which is pumped into a reactor where the liquid is converted to a vapor at 900 degrees. The vapor is emitted through a vent as a colorless and odorless gas. The sewage is disposed of. This system was developed by Ray Lore of Seaview Floating Homes, Miami, Florida. Another device, the "digester system" of waste disposal, operates on the principle of oxydation and biochemical digestion; it was developed by Naval Architects, Engineers, and Consultants of Fort Lauderdale, Florida. An "evaporative toilet system" which renders human waste into a sterile concentrate was developed by General American Transportation Corp. of Chicago, Illinois. And as a final example, Incinomode Sales Co. of Dallas, Texas has an electric incinerator-type toilet which reduces all human waste to water vapor and a completely inorganic bacteria-free mineral ash, which can literally be disposed of anywhere.

Looking ahead, the boat owner will be confronted by conflicting waste disposal device claims, along with diverse federal, state, and local pollution laws. The Boating Industry Associations note that the Federal Water Quality Improvement Act and its subsequent regulations on sewage discharge from boats won't take effect on federal waters for a minimum of two years for new boats and five years for existing ones. "Couple this with the fact that state and local governments are still free to enact their own measures, and are doing so, and you have a crazy-quilt pattern of laws and ordinances that can thwart even the richest, most law-abiding boat owner," said Ron Stone, Boating Industry Associations' government relations director. The association, 401 N. Michigan Ave., Chicago, Illinois 60611, issues an information kit, "Pollution and Pleasure Boats," containing a chart on state laws, information on shore pump-out equipment, copies of federal laws and regulations, and other background material. Contact Al Limburg for one.

7

The Houseboat
Ashore and Asea

A few more phases of houseboating are next discussed in order to help you become a better skipper or participant. Obviously, actual time at the helm is the best training of all, but perhaps some reading beforehand will enable you to ask intelligent questions of the waterfront experts, and along with that, some book and magazine reading will alert you to some of the blunders and follies that can be avoided.

ANCHORS AND ANCHORING PRINCIPLES

Among the many types of anchors available, three are best suited for the houseboat. They include: yachtsman's anchor, the patent Danforth and Northill, and the mushroom type. The traditional yachtsman's anchor is heavy, and once set firmly on the bottom is an effective holding device. The patent Danforth and Northill anchors are reliable in holding power under extreme wind and current conditions and on hard or soft bottoms. They are foldable and light, which make them the favorites of houseboaters.

Anchor lines of manila or nylon, ⅜ or ½ inch thick, are recommended, and to adequately meet holding needs they should measure 100 feet for a boat of 20 feet, and 150 feet for a boat in the 30- to 40-foot class. Manila rope is cheaper than nylon, which is tougher, and will stretch under strain, an advantage when an anchor is hung up.

Dropping anchor is just that, not a throwing action procedure. The houseboat is headed into the wind or current and the engine stopped. First the anchor is checked for proper attachment to a cleat, then it is gently lowered over the side, paying out the line until it becomes slack, indicating that the hook is on bottom. The current or wind backs the boat down slowly, permitting the flukes to dig in and hold, as you pay out more line to where you wish to be.

Anchoring principles indicate that the line should be 5 to 10 times the depth of the water for effective holding action. Tides that may raise the houseboat should be taken into consideration. Effective holding power is enhanced when the pull of the line is more horizontal than vertical. The terminal end of the anchor line should be a short length of chain that tends to keep the line from chafing and that keeps the anchor lying flat for better holding power.

In retrieving the anchor, the boat is driven at a slow speed in the direction of the paid-out line. The slack line is hauled in by a crew member, and when the boat is over the anchor, the line vertical, the crew member breaks it free from the bottom with a sharp heave on the line. The anchor is stored on deck in an accessible location as a safety measure. Should an engine fail, the anchor can be dropped immediately overboard to keep the boat from drifting into obstacles and to stabilize it for repairs, and the like.

In cruising unknown waters the anchorage should be in an area as protected as possible from the heaviest blow, tide, or current you are likely to encounter. Prevailing winds, the direction from which bad storms strike, should be known.

The holding power of an anchor is dependent upon the depth of water and the kind of bottom: sand, rocks, mud, weeds. Your chart indicates this, and beyond that, you can query local seamen for advice on specific questions, especially the direction of adverse winds.

On the Atlantic seaboard and the Great Lakes, most of the bad storms come from the east, southeast, and northeast. If at all possible, anchorages protected from these blows should be selected. Next, if there

The anchor must hold the boat securely, release quickly, and be snag-free. For retrieval, it is pulled in the opposite direction from which it was set. (Jerry Martin Co.)

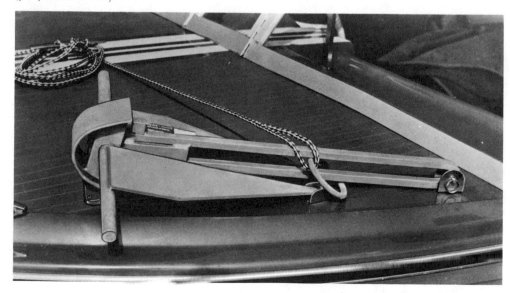

are neighbors, check the way their boats swing when the wind changes, the length of the anchor line, and the extremity of the circle. Select a position so that the other boat will swing clear of your boat and anchoring line.

In tight quarters, should there not be enough room for a swinging boat, an additional (stern) anchor can be dropped. Then balance the lengths of both anchor lines by taking up on the bow line while you let out the stern line. The boat is then stabilized midway between the two anchors.

LOCKS AND LOCKING THROUGH

A watercourse in its natural state racing down the land's declivity would restrict boating to a few isolated stretches of deep water. To make large rivers navigable along their entire course, in both flood and drought, engineers have placed dams at strategic places to create, in effect, a series of lakes and pools—the level of each succeeding downriver pool being lower than the one above it.

In conjunction with this stairway of pools, locks with watertight chambers and gates at each end provide the means for watercraft to ascend or descend from level to level. In cruising upstream to a higher pool, the houseboat enters the open downstream gate. After entry into the lock, the gates close, and water fills the lock until it reaches the upstream level. Then the upstream gate opens, the whistle blast gives the signal to motor out, and the voyage is continued at the new-found level.

Don't worry about locks; if you can navigate in tight places you are prepared to handle locking through. You may have to wait your turn, or go through with another boat, but that's up to the lockmaster. He is in charge of the river traffic and ready to help boaters in every way. Lockmasters are interesting people, especially the Canadians, who like to hear where you're headed and how far you've come, and engage in general gossip.

Lock construction varies in type and size, and each lock seems to have a character of its own. The modern trend is for fewer but larger locks on the big rivers. The new locks are 600 to 1,200 feet long and up to 110 feet wide, which approaches Panama Canal lock size. These large locks speed up river travel, and that's welcome news to the commercial and recreational boater. Negotiating a series of locks offers the houseboater a change of pace, especially on long cruises, and that is welcome.

In locking through, the houseboat must be protected from the concrete lock walls, and from other craft. To protect the boat sides from chafing, fenders are hung over the side; they come in many sizes, shapes, and designs: pieces of rope or wood, canvas bags stuffed with cork or hay, auto tires (illegal in some canals), and padded planks.

When the boat is in the lock and properly fendered, the next step is to tie a line to the bow of the boat, run it over the bollard, and bring it around a stern cleat, keeping the houseboat parallel to the lock wall.

LOCK OPERATION

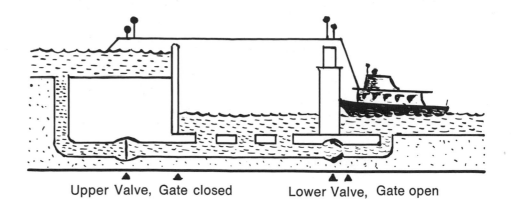

Upper Valve, Gate closed   Lower Valve, Gate open

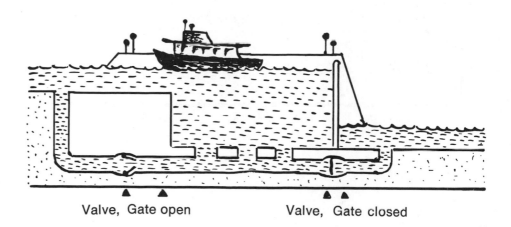

Valve, Gate open   Valve, Gate closed

The lock valves let the water in or out of the lock, and it is necessary to tend the line around the top bollard that controls the houseboat as it is raised or lowered.

At some locks, as the Chittenden Lock in Seattle, Washington, and along the St. Lawrence Waterway, it is possible to throw a line around the bollards, and when the water goes out, the tender removes the line and pitches it to the boat. At locks that are undermanned, there is no line release help, and the houseboater must be prepared to release from the stern cleat, running the free end around the bollard.

Canadian locks are set up to accommodate pleasure craft and have along lock walls closely spaced holds of chains, cables, or pipes which offer ideal control of boats without looping lines around bollards.

As a precaution of concern, sometimes a water valve is opened only on one side of the lock, and an unequal inflow produces a surge of water in the confined lock that can push boats against other boats or against the far wall. For that reason, prior to entering a lock, secure all movable objects to keep them from sliding about.

PROFILE OF ILLINOIS WATERWAY AND
THE TENNESSEE RIVER
(not to scale)

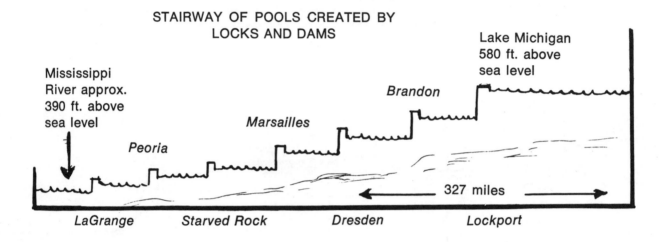

STAIRWAY OF POOLS CREATED BY
LOCKS AND DAMS

Lake Michigan
580 ft. above
sea level

Mississippi
River approx.
390 ft. above
sea level

Brandon

Marsailles

Peoria

327 miles

LaGrange   Starved Rock   Dresden   Lockport

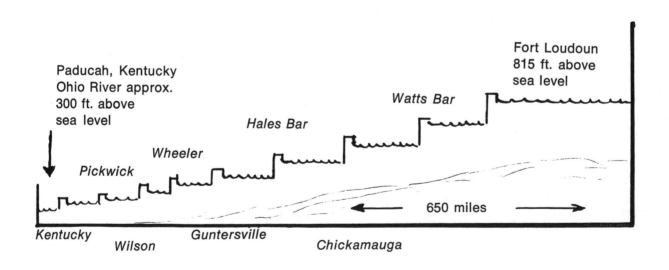

Fort Loudoun
815 ft. above
sea level

Paducah, Kentucky
Ohio River approx.
300 ft. above
sea level

Watts Bar

Hales Bar

Wheeler

Pickwick

650 miles

Kentucky   *Guntersville*
      Wilson   *Chickamauga*

A lesser used type of locking-through procedure is the railroad lock which consists of a flat car with handrails and a V-shaped cradle that keeps the boat upright and secure. The wheeled cradle is powered and runs over a track that connects two different bodies of water.

When locking through stateside waters, try to keep a pair of binoculars on the lock to ascertain what activity is evident. Sound your horn one mile distant from the lock, hoping for the lockmaster's response of flashing the green light for entry. A flashing red prohibits entry, while a flashing amber indicates a cautious preliminary approach. Most Canadian locks do not have light indicators, and boats are waved in by the lockmaster from the top of the lock.

Such locking systems as the Erie Canal's are governed by a time schedule: boats lock through on the hour going west, and on the half-hour going east. In the event of large numbers of boats going in one direction, the schedule is altered to accommodate the majority.

Some locks, as on the New York Barge Canal, have specific rules requiring boats to either tie up to a ladder or have 100 feet of line to reach from the bow of the boat up to the top of the lock and down to the stern of your boat. With experience, most skippers can get through most locks by holding or fending off with a boat hook. On the Erie Canal the speed limit is 10 miles an hour to minimize the wake on this narrow waterway.

Flotilla of cruisers is leaving Lock and Dam No. 18 on the Mississippi River above Burlington, Iowa. (Corps of Engineers, Rock Island, Illinois)

Most locks in use today are electrically operated, but some in the United States and Canada are operated by hand. Some lockmasters and attendants are required to perform maintenance and repairs around the locks and grounds. All of which means that the lock personnel may be busy with chores, and boaters will have to wait.

The houseboat skipper realizes that a precise schedule through many locks on heavily trafficked waters is impossible to maintain and that sometimes at the height of the summer cruising season the delay can be a whole day. He also knows that pleasure boats are not allowed in locks with gasoline barges or other boats with inflammable cargoes. He is also aware that there is a priority, established by the Secretary of the Army, with respect to the handling of traffic through locks. Precedence is in the following order:

1. U.S. military craft
2. Mail boats
3. Commercial passenger craft
4. Commercial tows
5. Commercial fishermen
6. Pleasure boats

In summary, the Corps of Engineers lists these locking rules. Before using navigation locks be sure you:

1. Know the rules and regulations governing the use of navigation locks.
2. Have at least 50 feet of mooring line.
3. Have a mooring ring or similar device on your boat.
4. Require passengers to remain seated during lockage.
5. Wear life jacket when handling lines on deck.
6. Obey all instructions given by lockmaster.
7. Travel at reduced speeds when entering and leaving.
8. Have fenders to save damage to boat.

BARGES ON BIG RIVERS

Most of our navigable rivers handle considerable commercial traffic, and the houseboater should give these working boats a wide berth. The huge barges pushed ahead by powerful towboats frequently exceed 1,000 feet in length and can be as much as 200 feet wide. Once underway they cannot be maneuvered sharply or stopped quickly. They may require as much as a half mile when a very large and heavy tow is involved. No houseboater can be sure that his engine will not stall at any given time and should therefore allow himself plenty of leeway when crossing in front of a tow in order to avoid endangering himself, his passengers and his craft.

The same danger threat applies to water skiers, who could tumble or be thrown from their skis at any moment. Some skiers have even tried to go between the barges in a tow with fatal results. The very presence on a waterway of vessels as big as towboats and barges creates danger. The suction or undertow around such massive craft, whether they are in motion or standing still, is a strong and dangerous force.

In nighttime travel on the major rivers, towboats and barges can be menaces. Only a red and green navigation light and a small amber warning light are required. Some tows can be ¼ mile long, with the lights so far apart that a skipper can easily assume there is nothing but water in between. To complicate matters, fully laden barges ride low in the water and blend with the shoreline. Many pleasure boating groups have suggested to the Coast Guard the use of reflective tape running along the sides of barges, or lights every 20 feet along the length and breadth of the tow, and also a string of lights with the flashing sequence that produces a streaking effect similar to those of airport landing strips.

MOORING THE HOUSEBOAT

The ever-present problem of a houseboat owner is parking it between cruises and between seasons. The alternatives include: a mooring, slip, rack, or trailer.

Mooring consists of a float or buoy anchored by chain or line to which the houseboat ties. A dinghy is used to transfer crew from shore to mooring. Some marinas offer dinghy service, otherwise the houseboater must use his own—carrying it topside, towing it, or keeping it secured to the buoy when asea.

Approaching a mooring is easier than coming to anchorage at a dock. The mooring is best approached at a slow speed from the downwind or down-current side. As the buoy is reached a crew member reaches over the side and hauls the buoy, pennant, and mooring eye onto the deck. On houseboats with a high freeboard, a boat hook is used. The mooring eye is engaged and immediately placed over the bow cleat, and a shift into reverse stops any forward momentum of the boat. Most houseboat

USE OF BOLLARD

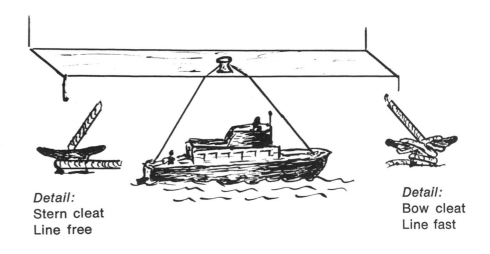

Detail:
Stern cleat
Line free

Detail:
Bow cleat
Line fast

A high-riding buoy with reflective blue stripe is easy to locate, and simplifies the job of mooring a boat. (Jerry Martin Co.)

forward decks are low enough for the skipper to see the buoy and check his approach; otherwise it is necessary to get help, via hand signals, from a crew member on the foredeck.

In leaving a mooring, the procedure is reversed: After the line has been freed, the buoy is dropped over the side, and the boat is backed downwind or down current until the skipper sees the buoy. A shift to forward, carefully avoiding the buoy, gets you underway.

Slip Mooring is ideal in that it offers an individual parking stall formed by floats, pilings, or walls, set out from the pier or wharf. Loading and unloading, embarking and debarking are possible from a firm footing on the boat. The slip is ideal in a protected harbor, as four lines, two to each side, secure the houseboat without fenders. If four lines cannot be used, spring lines can be substituted. They run from the amidships cleat on the houseboat to the dock cleat forward and aft. The spring lines reduce movement caused by wake waves and wind. Fenders are used, and in tidal waters both lines and fenders must be adequate to compensate for the rising and falling water levels caused by the tide.

Boat Rack storage represents a dry land mooring where a fork lift tractor-type vehicle lifts the boat and stores it on a rack that is generally roofed, sometimes enclosed—an expensive but secure type of mooring.

Trailering the Houseboat. Disappointed by the failure of finding a marina mooring or slip, many boat owners are forced to trailer their craft, towing and launching them every time they are used. In truth, many have come to appreciate the nuisance. The advantages of returning a boat to the back yard or driveway include better security against theft and vandalism. Also, the boat is always at hand, so that you can use spare time in cleaning, scraping, painting, polishing, decorating, cleaning the interior, and tuning up the engine. There are many factors involved in matching the houseboat to the trailer: maximum load limits, balance, proper springs, tie-downs, hitch, brakes, and lights. The manufacturer, or seller, of your houseboat is the best source of information for all aspects of trailering it.

The above-mentioned marine-offered storage possibilities are ideal in that most services desired by the houseboat owner are conveniently localized. Along with storage and mooring, there are a repair shop, pump-out station, groceries, water, ice, fuel, and other services and supplies. Important too, for many, is that you'll be clustered with houseboaters of kindred bent to exchange yarns and information on boats, places, and people. Other than privately owned marinas, mooring and storage applications are made through the town or city Harbor Master. Be prepared for a long wait, for all across the country boats exceed the available mooring and slip space.

DOCKING THE HOUSEBOAT

Docking is not easy at first. You must know the responsiveness of your craft, how much room it requires to turn a given number of de-

DOCKING

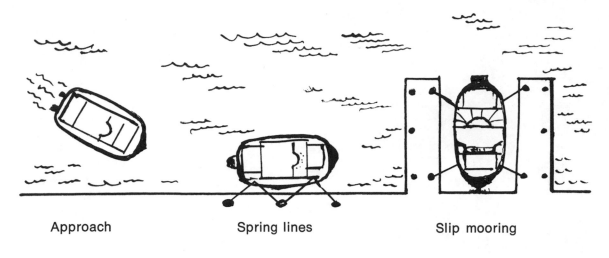

Approach   Spring lines   Slip mooring

grees, how to use lines and shore help, and how to train crew members to offer proper help. Confidence in tight maneuvering comes from a lot of practice.

In leaving a dock it is recommended that before starting the engine, you study the wind, current, and congestion factors, noting possible hazards and forces that will affect the progress of the boat, and what steering compensations must be made. The pivot point of a houseboat is near the middle forward of amidships; therefore, a quick turn of the bow will not allow for the stern to come around and clear the dock side. Ideally, you back straight out for approximately two boat lengths, so that the boat will clear when you shift forward and make the hard turn seaward.

In congested conditions, the turning can be improved by keeping the bow line secured to the dock, while the stern is turned away (seaward). The bow line is then cast off, and there's room to back up into open water. Once clear of the dock and other boats, the engine is shifted into forward gear.

In approaching a dock, the first concern is to ascertain the strength of the tide, wind, and/or current. Begin a shallow angle 30-to-45-degree approach about 30 yards off the dock, with just enough power to assure control. Dock lines and fenders must be in place, ready for use. The engine is shifted into neutral about a boat length from the dock. Once the dock is reached, the boat is trimmed alongsides and the lines secured.

A favorable wind blowing toward the dock enables the skipper to cut the engine several feet from, and parallel to, the dock and allow the wind to ease the boat into the dock.

An example of auxiliary craft being towed, carried topside, and lashed alongside on Lake Cumberland in Kentucky.

USE OF AUXILIARY CRAFT

There are many times when the houseboater will take along a small boat, dinghy, canoe, or inflatable raft. Once the houseboat is anchored, the use of the small craft permits extensive probing of coves, feeder streams, and shallow waters with snags that are inaccessible to larger craft.

Inflatable rafts and canoes can be carried on deck, but some skippers prefer to tow auxiliary craft. The towline of ¼- to ½-inch line is secured to a stern cleat; or use two stern cleats with a bridle between them for attachment of the line. The towed craft should be secured low at the bow to permit it to ride high. A bridle encircling the bow area and attached near the keel by the towing line makes an efficient tow. There should be enough line so that the towed craft rides just forward of the crest of the first or second stern wave. If the towed boat yaws (weaves from side to side), increase the line length, place some ballast in its stern, and experiment at different speeds.

BEACHING THE HOUSEBOAT

By virtue of design and hull construction, houseboats, except those with inboard engines, can be beached to good advantage; this eliminates the problem of searching for a marina dock or mooring. Select the idyllic or shaded bank, and before hitting the beach, shut off the motor, tip it up, and coast in. Never ram a houseboat onto the shore under power. A crew member or two steps over the side, checks the nature of the water's bottom, and, if it's acceptable, eases the boat onto the beach. Before getting into your activities ashore and dispersing over the land, there's the consideration of tides, if you're on tidal waters, and wakes from large boats, if you're on a big river. Embarrassment may come from being left high and dry because of an outgoing tide, or lifted onto jagged rocks or floated against a bridge because of extensive wakes. Caution: Do not beach your houseboat on mudflats or other soft bottoms, where it will be difficult to back, push, or motor off.

Sometimes, instead of beaching, the skipper may decide to anchor offshore with an additional line leading to a shore tie or by using two anchors. In anchoring offshore, the stern anchor is first dropped and the bow nosed toward the shore, while a crewman takes the bowline and secures it on shore. For proper trim and position, the anchor and bow lines are taken up, or let out, then secured so that the boat rests in sufficient water depth for its draft needs. Using two anchors was discussed above under "Anchors and Anchoring Principles."

TOWING A DISTRESSED BOAT

The Federal Boat Safety Act makes it mandatory "to aid a vessel in trouble, so long as it doesn't endanger your own safety or craft." But even before it was mandatory to help, there has been, through the centuries, an "unwritten law" of the sea to aid another in distress or disabled. Today, that assistance may take many forms: a gallon of gas, enough to enable a boater to reach shore; supplying tools, equipment, or just plain waterway advice; or, more dramatically, rescuing the occupants of a capsized craft. In any emergency the true seaman does not turn his back on a fellow boatman. Assistance on the water is a two-way street; both parties should understand how to safely offer and receive help and lessen the chances of further damage or injury.

Proper towing requires a few basic procedures that should be followed by both skippers. The tow line is attached securely to the disabled boat, but in a manner that will enable immediate release if the line becomes too strained and in danger of breaking. The towline should be attached to a fitting of the disabled vessel that is bolted to the keel or to a bridle that is passed around the hull for effectiveness and less damage in towing. The skipper doing the towing should attach the towline to the forward-most position possible on his craft. A line attached to the stern would prevent maneuvering and create an extreme drag, which could result in a swamping if the conditions became rough.

Ample chafing precautions are necessary, as much strain is placed on the line as it rubs against bitts and chocks and across rails. Towels, dish rags, and oil cloths tied in place with strong cord will help. Nylon or plastic water ski lines, which have excellent spring and flotation, or a thick manila line would be good examples of proper towing lines.

Starting off easily, the tow boat should maintain a steady, not jerky, pull on the vessel in tow. Occupants of both boats should keep watchful eyes on the towline. If it breaks loose, the whiplash may cause injury.

The line holds, the towing progress is slow but adequate, and you bring the distressed boat to dock. "Good show," you say, but the whole matter of towing a disabled vessel is a highly controversial matter. All of the above is possible only if the weather conditions are ideal, the towline adequate, the power sufficient, the distance short, and so forth, and so on.

Realistically considered, the towing of a disabled craft is a most precarious undertaking: the towline must be approximately 3 inches in circumference, 300 feet long, and in good condition—which is seldom true of an accessory equipment item; also, a proper towing attachment, such as one bolted to the keel, is a rarity in houseboats. Most likely, the emergency arose in darkness, fog, stormy seas, or dashing or strong waves; and the towing precedure would not be so pat. Also, more honestly, an extremely taut towline could break and whip across the flat houseboat deck and break arms or legs and fracture skulls.

The prudent skipper, coming upon a towing situation, would be within the spirit of the Federal Boat Safety Act if he concerned himself with the endangered crew and left the salvage work to professionals. The whole matter is akin to any accident-injury circumstance. After administering first aid, you make great efforts to get the victim to a doctor as soon as possible and relinquish the responsibility to a more competent person. So too with a disabled vessel, for as soon as you get the Coast Guard or local marine patrol involved you're home free— the responsibility ends.

ROPES AND KNOTS

Ropes and Lines. First of all, a rope is called "a rope" when it is in a coil in the dealer's stockroom. Once aboard a boat, a length of rope becomes "a line"—as anchor line, dock line, bow line, stern line, and the like. Rope types include the natural: manila, sisal, and cotton; and synthetic: nylon, dacron, polyethylene, and polypropylene. Manila is by far the best natural fiber rope because of its strength, durability, and tying and splicing suppleness. The main advantages of synthetic ropes over the natural fiber types are strength and protection from rot and mildew. Nylon, for example, has a breaking strain twice that of same size manila, but it is heavier and more expensive. Some synthetic ropes are unusual in that they gain rather than lose strength when wet, and that, along with their elasticity, makes them ideal for the houseboat skipper.

Knots. The welfare of a crew and boat may depend upon a skipper's ability to tie a few basic knots efficiently and quickly. These few knots, each designed for a definite purpose, should be included in the skills of every houseboater. He should be proficient enough to tie them in the dark, behind his back, and even underwater.

A youngster can tie a nondescript knot that will hold adequately, but the important question is, can it be untied quickly? Which brings up the requirements of a good knot. The knot should be easily tied, fit a specific need, hold adequately, and untie quickly.

BASIC KNOTS

Reef, or square knot

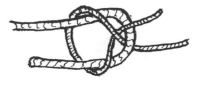

Sheet bend or weaver's knot

Clove hitch

Two half hitches

Bowline in three steps

The houseboater will need to make a line fast to a cleat, post, piling, bitt, or ring; tie it into a loop; or join it with another line of equal or unequal size. A few knots are required for these situations, and knowing them indicates that you're on your way to becoming a sailor. Essential ones are:

Reef knot for joining two lines of equal diameter

Weaver's knot for joining lines of unequal diameter

WHIPPING ROPE

Make loop,

Wrap line,

Pull to bury ends, snip

CLEAT HITCH

Complete turn around base,

Around horn,

Once again

Half-hitch knot for making fast to a ring bolt

Clove hitch for making fast to a post or round object

Bowline for making an unslippable eye or loop in the end of the line

Cleat tie for making fast a line around base and horns of a cleat and securing it

Whipping rope (A sign of a good skipper is to have all line ends whipped, taped, or twine wrapped; cowtail or bushy, unraveled ends are inexcusable.)

The quickest way to whip rope is to tape the ends with waterproof adhesive tape. The most efficient and longer lasting method is by coiling twine around the end of the line. In whipping synthetic rope, use heat from an open flame to fuse the end fibers and strands solidly together.

8

Essential and
Optional Equipment

There are many equipment items, optional accessories, and gadgets that are available to the houseboater. His first concern, however, should be those required by law (the Motor Boat Act of 1940); secondly, those concerned with safety, and finally those that are offered for comfort.

Certain houseboat equipment is prescribed by law—federal, state, or both. The jurisdiction of the government (U.S. Coast Guard) is confined to navigable waters, which include most of the areas of participation of the houseboater: both oceans, the Gulf of Mexico, the Great Lakes, major rivers, and so on.

The non-navigable waters, mostly land-locked lakes lying wholly within the boundaries of one state, are governed by the local authority, usually the state, that determines what equipment is necessary. Individual states can specify equipment so long as it does not negate federal standards. A brief description of essential items is here noted.

ESSENTIAL EQUIPMENT

Alarm Systems. Adequate warning devices that indicate dangerous conditions such as excessive presence of fumes, water in the bilge, engine overheating, low oil pressure, and similar dangers are required on houseboats powered by engines over 10 horsepower.

Cleaning Supplies. Sponges, rags, mop, and bucket are necessary for

RUNNING LIGHTS

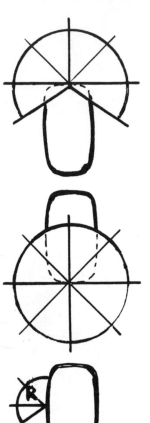

A 20-point bow light from dead ahead
to 2-points abaft the beam on both sides.

A 32-point white stern light that shows
all around the circle of the horizon.

A 10-point red port side light that shows
dead ahead to 2-points abaft the port beam.

A 10-point green starboard side light that
shows dead ahead to 2-points abaft the
starboard beam.

The red and green lights show red from
dead ahead to 2-points abaft the port
beam, and green in like value scope for the
starboard side.

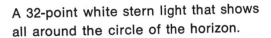

proper housekeeping and keeping decks, bilges, and engine area ship-shape.

Compass. The compass is essential for navigation, especially in fog, strange waters, rain, poor visibility, and in traversing large expanses of water.

Deck Lines. Manila or nylon lines are required for securing the houseboat fore and aft, for spring lines, and for anchoring. Nylon has higher elasticity than other synthetics and therefore can act as its own shock absorber when the boat pitches and rocks at its mooring.

Fire Extinguishers. Federal law requires houseboats under 26 feet in length to carry one fire extinguisher, boats 26 to 40 feet to carry two, and boats over 40 feet to carry three; modern fire extinguishers using foam carbon dioxide or a dry chemical are preferred.

Insurance statistics indicate that fires on boats occur mostly in the galley and the fuel compartment. Mount your extinguishers in these areas.

Flame Arrester. This device, attached to the air intakes of carburetors of gasoline engines, prevents backfire. Flame arresters must have flame-tight connections, clean elements, and no separation of grid elements which would permit flames to bypass the grid elements.

Fume Detectors. A detection device (alarm system) with a "sensing" component below, connected to a buzzer, bell, or light that is activated when fumes are present.

Lifesaving Devices. Life preservers of kapok, fibrous glass, or uni-cellular plastic foam are acceptable flotation material, as are the design styles of jacket, bib, vest, cushion, or ring buoy. One is required for each passenger aboard. Coast Guard-approved life preservers bear markings showing flotation material used, size, and approval number. The advantage of a ring life buoy is that it can be thrown a distance to a person overboard. All buoys are fitted with a length of strong bright-colored floating-type grab line.

The 360-degree light on a mast adds a decorative ond functional option for a houseboat. (Bremer Mfg. Co.)

Note: Buoyant vests provide less buoyancy than do life preservers, and they are not legally acceptable on houseboats over 40 feet in length, or on vessels carrying passengers for hire.

Light Requirements. From sunset to sunrise, a houseboat's lights must be displayed to announce its presence and/or direction of travel. Houseboats under 26 feet must carry forward a combination red-and-green bow light arranged to show red on the port side and green on the starboard side. Each colored light shows through 10 points from dead ahead to 2 points abaft the beam on its respective side. A white light is carried aft, arranged higher than the red and green lights, showing all around the circle (or horizon) for 32 points. For handy and precise reference the Coast Guard regulations call for the point system which encompasses the entire circle around a vessel. A point is equal to 11¼ degrees, therefore a full circle (360 degrees) equals 32 points. See diagram for visual clarification.

Lights prescribed for houseboats above the 26-foot class are slightly different from the above. Forward they carry a 20-point white bow light showing from dead ahead to 2 points abaft the beam on either side. The port side carries a separate red 10-point light that shows from dead ahead to 2 points abaft the port beam. The starboard green 10-point light shows from dead ahead to 2 points abaft the starboard beam. A 32-point aft white light shows all around the circle and is higher than the white bow light.

The red and green side lights must be fitted with inboard screens, mounted on the cabin sides so that the lights will not show across the bow. This is mostly controlled by unique construction that confines the light beam to prescribed point values. Every white light must be visible at least 2 miles, every colored light, at least 1 mile.

■ **Lighting (Auxiliary).** A source of light entirely independent of the houseboat's electrical system should be provided. A beacon-type search- or flashlight, complete with extra batteries and bulbs, should be provided and available at all times.

Numbering (for Identification) Requirements. The Federal Boating Act establishes a uniform numbering system for the identification of pleasure craft, called "Certificate of Number." Houseboats are numbered by the state in which the boat is principally used, or if on coastal waters, the state in which the boat is usually docked, moored, and stored. State fees, approximately $3, are fixed by state law and are valid for 3 years. Information about your state's numbering system is available from the Secretary of State, Coast Guard, or marine dealers.

There are exceptions. If a houseboat is used primarily on navigable waters in New Hampshire, Washington, Alaska, or the District of Columbia, the Certificate of Number will be issued by the Coast Guard. Application forms are available at post offices and Coast Guard facilities of the above states involved. Applications with a fee of $3 are made to: Commandant (FA-1) U.S. Coast Guard, Washington D.C. 20226.

■ **Display of Number.** Your identifying number must be painted on, or attached to each side of, the forward half of the vessel, and no conflicting number may be displayed thereon. Numbers must be in block characters, read from left to right, be of a color contrasting with the background, and be not less than 3 inches in height. The correct form using block letters, properly spaced, will appear as DC-3577-AB. The use of script letters, *DC-3577-AB,* and letters and numbers crowded together, DC3577AB, are incorrect.

■ **Transfer of Number.** Upon sale or other transfer of boat, where the vessel will continue to be used in the same state, the original number will be issued to the new owner. Numbers may not be transferred from one houseboat to another. If the state of principal use is changed, the owner must make application for a number in the new state and surrender the old Certificate of Number within 90 days.

Pump. For bailing out water and throwing it overboard, the lightweight plastic pump, with hose connection, keeps the boat dry and stable.

Spare Fuel Tank. An extra fuel tank is necessary for that margin of safety when strong winds, tides, or current eat up more gas than anticipated. It's surprising how often running out of gas is an embarrassing predicament.

Auxiliary lighting by a propane lantern utilizes disposable cartridges and provides instant, safe light. (Coleman Co.)

Ventilators. At least two ventilator ducts fitted with cowls for the purpose of properly and efficiently ventilating the bilges of every engine and fuel tank compartment of boats using gasoline, or other fuel of a flashpoint less than 110 degrees Fahrenheit, are required.

Whistle, Horn, or Bell. All houseboats must carry a suitable sounding device to give both passing signals and fog signals. On small boats the whistle or horn may be hand-, mouth-, or power-operated and must be audible for at least ½ mile. On larger boats the signaling device must be audible at least a mile. Houseboats over 26 feet in length must have also an efficient bell that is used when the boat is at anchor in a fog, and capable of producing a clear, full bell-like tone.

OPTIONAL EQUIPMENT

The number of optional accessories that a houseboater will buy is tied up with the nature of cruising plans, living aboard, the hobby interests of his family, various individual and group activities, and many, many other reasons peculiar to each individual.

A wet bar may be important to one houseboater, anathema to another. The provision for an adequate powder room, and privacy, will always be a female requisite of high priority. The aft deck rigged for deep-sea fishing will be popular with many; others will prefer the flying bridge as worth the extra expense; ditto for air conditioning. There will be a wide divergence of opinion regarding such options as a tinted windshield, cigarette lighter, automatic anchor hoist, ice cube maker, automatic pilot, deep freeze, and so on.

Obviously, the houseboater on a tight budget will do without many extras. Yet he must go far beyond the essential equipment, discussed above, as federal regulations do not touch all the bases. There is no provision, or requirement, for such inherent needs as an anchor, compass, first-aid kit, fenders, or tool kit, to name a few. The type and number of options a houseboater will buy is strictly a personal judgment. Listed below are several, with descriptions, to help you make that judgment.

Anchor. A device that engages the bottom of a waterway, and restricts the movement of a houseboat, represents an important option. Preferred are the lightweight types such as Danforth, Northill, and mushroom models.

Barometer. Insight into weather conditions by measuring pressure exerted by the atmosphere is possible through the use of an aneroid barometer. It can be as small as a pocket watch, but for ease of reading and for greater accuracy, the clock size is better. Barometers are not expensive; pay what you would for a reliable watch.

Binoculars. The 7 × 50 center focus is considered the best all-around marine binocular. The more powerful models require a tripod for steadying. Glasses are handy for the observation of buoys and other navigation aids along cruising routes and for wildlife watching too.

Boat Hook. A slender pole of aluminum or plastic, 4 to 7 feet long, is needed for picking up lines, fending off lock walls or piers, and when coming alongside.

Capacity Plate. Many houseboat manufacturers display a plate inside their boats showing recommended weight capacity usually in the number of persons, as well as in the number of pounds. These are only recommended values for fair weather and do not relieve the skipper of the responsibility for exercising individual judgment. In the absence of a capacity plate, the skipper guards against overloading of passengers and gear, distributes the load evenly, and keeps it low. The movement of people aboard, the conditions of water and wind, and the destination should be taken into consideration.

Cooler. The insulated box that keeps drinks and food cool during summer outings, and warm for winter activities, has become a traditional piece of equipment for all outdoor people. For the houseboater, it serves both aboard the boat as an extra ice cube supply and an adjunct to ease an overcrowded refrigerator, and on shore as a handy container that keeps the Coke and beer cool.

Depth Sounder. This electronic instrument gauges the distance between the houseboat and any variation in the water bottom, sand bar, ledge, rocks, a wreck, or a school of fish. This valuable aid, also called a fish locator, enables the fishermen aboard to know just how far to drop lures and bait. Once a school of fish is located, all the rods aboard are brought into action, and the menu will be supplemented with fresh fish. Treasure hunters also find the depth sounder a valuable aid to their explorations.

Coolers for drinks and food have developed into "must" items for outdoor-active people. (Thermos and Coleman Cos.)

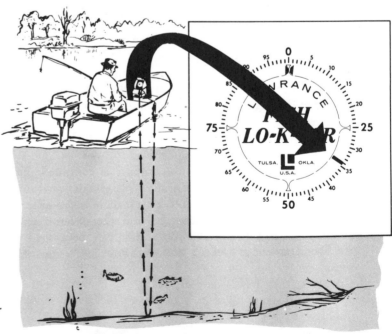

Principles of a depth finder

LO-K-TOR BOTH SENDS AND RECEIVES SIGNALS.
RECEIVED SIGNALS ARE INDICATED ON DIAL.

Engine Parts (Spare). Extra parts like spark plugs, coil, condenser, distributor points, gasket material, and wire and tape, along with suitable tools, should be aboard.

Fender. Any shock-absorbing material or device that is hung over the side of a houseboat to protect it against chafe is a must. Wood, rubber, or plastic fenders protect the finish of topsides when docking, locking, coming alongside, or when tying up to other boats.

First-Aid Kit. The emergency kit in a waterproof rattle-free case, secured in a convenient place, known and available to all adult crew members, must be adequately provisioned: bandages, tape, healing ointments, lotions, personal prescription medicines, and the like. First-aid treatment and simple remedies for sea sickness, nausea, diarrhea, heat exhaustion, sunstroke, and shock should be known. The Red Cross

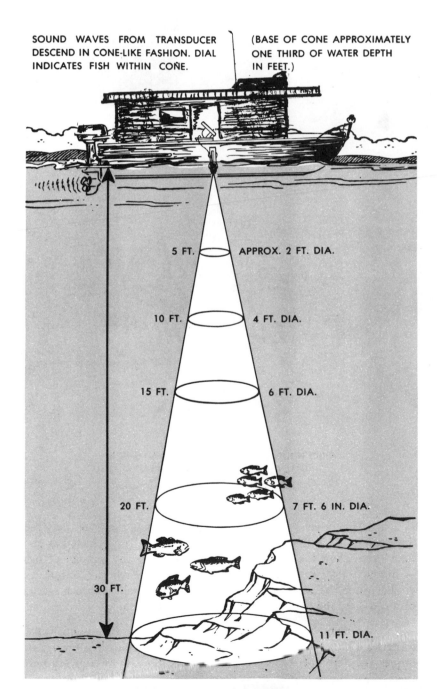

SOUND WAVES FROM TRANSDUCER DESCEND IN CONE-LIKE FASHION. DIAL INDICATES FISH WITHIN CONE.

(BASE OF CONE APPROXIMATELY ONE THIRD OF WATER DEPTH IN FEET.)

Principles of a depth finder

5 FT.   APPROX. 2 FT. DIA.

10 FT.   4 FT. DIA.

15 FT.   6 FT. DIA.

20 FT.   7 FT. 6 IN. DIA.

30 FT.

11 FT. DIA.

ABOVE: *Fenders hung over sides of docked houseboats protect them against chafe.* LEFT: *This flying bridge has a pie-shape R-T antenna which improves ship-to-shore radiotelephone communications. (Vorta Systems, Inc.)*

first-aid manual should be a part of the kit. A good procedure is to query a local doctor as to what the contents of the kit should be, for a health problem afloat on the Great Lakes may be different than one in the Caribbean Sea.

Flares. For summoning aid in emergencies, the skyrocket type flare is ideal. It comes in its own waterproof container, a little larger than a fountain pen, and is readily discharged. Other methods of indicating distress include: repeated raising and lowering of one's outstretched arms, continuous sounding of horn or whistle, an orange smoke signal, continuous red flare, and burning tar or oil in a fireproof container.

Flying Bridge. The up-forward location of a flying bridge makes for better vision and maneuverability of your boat, which enhances control of the houseboat at all times. The position of the bridge, besides offering good visibility from the forward position, should give a sufficient view aft to provide a frame of reference for proper steering, speed, and control. Close-channel navigation, docking, coming alongside, and similar procedures are easy operations for the skipper with a flying bridge. This option doesn't come cheap, as all instrumentation and controls must be duplicated above.

Foul Weather Gear. A small inventory of extra waterproof gear should be stowed aboard the houseboat. Guests will appreciate the jackets, hoods, trousers, tarps, and ponchos when the weather turns bad. With such protection, many times activities do not have to be postponed.

Intercom. The intercom, priced as low as $100, besides offering an interior communication system with microphone and speakers, can be plugged in and switched to serve as a hailer when the skipper wishes to communicate with another boat, the dock, or a distant person.

Ladder. For the crew members who leave the houseboat for swimming, scuba diving, snorkeling, or water skiing, the ladder of 3, 4, or 5 steps makes reboarding an easy matter. Collapsible models with solid steps, banded together with strong rope, fold up when not in use and require little storage space.

Lines. Spare, unused lines of manila or nylon are often needed for anchors, dock lines, spring lines, and other general use.

Megaphone. There are two types: the economical cheerleader type of tough fiberboard with plastic mouthpiece, and the transistorized portable megaphone that delivers clear, distortion-free sound over a ½-mile distance.

Portable Radio. A must for the teen-agers in the crew, this is also very important for hearing whether forecasts.

Radar. The radar unit is an expensive instrument, used mostly on large houseboats for detection of hazards in heavy fog and darkness.

Rear-View Mirror. Enhances visibility to 360 degrees; it is important when towing water skiers or when navigating in tight places.

Speedometer. This is a necessary piece of equipment that serves as a means of checking engine performance and also knowing speeds in posted areas like harbors and in narrow channels with "No Wake" signs. You can use the trip recorder to indicate distance traveled and when to change course. After each leg of the trip, the mileage indicator is set back to zero, then checked for desired distances on the route.

Tent. The Pop-tent as optional equipment is ideal aboard the houseboat, in that it can be set up on deck or cabin top to provide an extra bedroom, dressing room for swimmers, or an emergency head, discussed below. Pop-tents are completely self-contained with their own poles, screened window and door, and a built-in floor. Once set up, the tent can be lifted and moved, and after a damp night it can be turned on its side and the underside dried.

The Pop-tent serves as an extra bedroom, a dressing room, and for other ship or shore uses. (Thermos Co.)

Toilet (Extra). No matter how many heads a houseboat is equipped with, there's always a jam-up at the facility. An extra head, economical and efficient, can be added by the use of a Pop-tent and a self-contained portable toilet with manual-pump flushing system. No external power or plumbing hook-up are required. Place the portable head in the tent, and label it "Emergency Head." After the need subsides, the tent can be struck, and easily stowed away. Also, should a lengthy stay on land be in the plans, the emergency head can serve well, especially on small islands.

Tool Kit. For trouble-shooting small problems take along pliers, screwdrivers, spark plugs, tape, rope, and so on.

Troller. A specialized attachment to a lure will plane the bait at a given depth where the coho, salmon and deep-sea species are feeding.

9

Family and
Retirement
Houseboating

There's a "Swiss Family Robinson" type of experience for youngsters in a houseboat. They are well provisioned and safe from the elements, and they engage in meaningful chores, exploring on land, and fishing asea. Anchored in a sheltered scenic cove, the junior crew members experience the pleasures of an old-fashioned "swimming hole" or, on shore, roving at will without the restraint of "No Trespassing" signs.

Conditioning the children to houseboat life calls for early exposure, tempered with caution: a day trip, then an overnighter in good weather to scenic waters, with some time on land, perhaps lunch. The maiden voyage will serve to check out both the craft and the reaction of the first mate (wife) and crew (children). The transition from the land-based home to houseboat living does not require extreme adjustment. The confinement of the craft is not too restrictive to ship and shore activities, and the moderate speed offers the pleasure of cruising. Security is good, in that parents can look through picture windows to spot children, who are always nearby and within hailing distance.

The houseboat offers early exposure to outdoor experiences to young children without such difficulties as living outside, setting up a shelter, gathering firewood, sleeping on the ground, hauling water, and using primitive sanitary facilities. The skipper, too, is pleased because he gets a cook and housekeeper and several hands in the deal, along with a semblance of back-home niceties.

Roughing it in comfort is what a houseboat vacation is. This new look in family vacation has many advantages: Even in the most remote area, you are housed in a structure that gives protection from the elements and bugs; there's a delightful combination of indoor/outdoor living, and after a day of activity, a shower before dinner, which is a sit-down affair at a table. In the evening the children can watch TV, play musical instruments, then sleep in comfortable beds, while parents enjoy a quiet neighbor- and child-free evening by themselves.

THE WOMAN'S ANGLE

The first mate, wife or mother, realizes that with today's spacious houseboats, she can live quite comfortably on water. Clothing is stored in closets, fishing tackle and gear in storage boxes, and food in the refrigerator.

Cooking is no problem, as many houseboats are equipped with such modern appliances as the eye-level oven, three-burner stove, rotisserie,

Family groups on Kentucky Lake in the western corner of the state returning from a shore picnic and barbecue.

and adequate work space. An electric radar oven is available as an option, and electric outlets are provided for toaster, coffee maker, and other appliances. There's no worry about pots and pans tipping over, as the floating kitchen is equipped with rails that hold pots in place in the roughest seas. In addition, there's sleeping space for all, a head, shower, and powder room; and beyond these, for the first mate there's the sharing of experiences with husband and children that wins her over every time.

ACTIVITIES FOR CHILDREN

Is there in the land a family vacation proposal so ideal, as planned and financed by parents, that it will receive the enthusiastic and thankful approval of their children? Definitely not! However, houseboating comes close. Here's why:

1. There are many challenging activities tailored to the level of each crew member.
2. Some treats remain the same, as the home-from-school cookies-and-milk reception by mother.
3. The basics of food, clothing, and shelter are not too different from what the youngsters left at home.

To help parents surreptitiously give children what's good for them, here are some guiding principles that will hopefully convince them to go along. After all, who wants to pay a baby-sitter for two weeks?

1. Don't delineate too rigid a program of activities, mileage, and destination.
2. Get all the children in on the planning, and consider each suggestion.
3. If possible, allow children to take along their best friends.
4. Once underway, give over completely the responsibility of certain aspects of the venture—for example, caring for pets, oiling fishing reels, storing rods, catching bait, dropping anchor, suggesting menus, and so on.
5. All assignments should be within a child's interest range and ability.
6. Don't be overly protective, preventing a child from the exhilarating experience of testing his own potential.

SUGGESTED PROGRAM ACTIVITIES

If you've ever made a game of learning road signs while traveling in a car, you can do the same aboard the houseboat. Make a game of

Invite junior crew members, of compatible age with your children, to share boating experiences. (Lazy Days)

learning the various buoys and markers, shouting them out by their name or message. Or have children keep count of how many boats of different shapes and sizes they see. This activity should keep children content for a while, and in the process they'll be learning about boats —an important factor in developing future seamen.

Many children relish the opportunity to sit in the skipper's chair, with you standing by to keep them out of trouble, of course. It's a thrill they won't soon forget.

If the child is old enough, put him to work. Children can serve as a lookout for floating debris, other boats, and channel markers. Other tasks include coiling lines, taking in fenders, polishing light lenses, and so on. Naturally, the older the child, the more responsibility he can accept, and, hopefully, the more anxious he'll be to go boating again.

When it's time to paint or shape up the boat, let the youngsters help. When they see you enjoying all aspects of boating, they'll get a better understanding of the sport, and develop a sense of responsibility toward their craft—again, hopefully.

Children are curious, and that trait should be forever nourished and developed. All types of nature guides should be included in the houseboat library so that questions on flora and fauna of a given region can be answered.

Rainy- or layover-day activities can include quiet reading, table games, cards, knitting, watching TV, or listening to records or tapes. The older, more responsible offspring can tidy up the decks, repair fishing tackle, and polish brass and table tops.

The auxiliary craft, canoe or dinghy, comes in handy for a run into town or the nearest marina for fill-in groceries or other essentials. This chore can be entrusted to older, responsible children. Involve them too with such grown-up tasks as docking, navigating, and perhaps a stint at the wheel.

Swimming is essential to boaters, instilling confidence in all water-related pursuits. Therefore, permit children at every opportunity to get acquainted with, and develop a love for, the water. The endurance type of skill is preferred over fancy strokes and speed swimming.

In South Sea Island cultures, where the food supply comes largely from the netting of fish, parents encourage their children to play cat's cradle, an intricate game played with a string looped over the fingers and, sometimes, transferred to another player so as to form designs. The game teaches dexterity that will enable them to better man the fish nets from an outrigger canoe in all types of waves. In effect, the mastery of simple game skills has a survival value, for the incompetent could get tangled in the nets or perhaps be pulled overboard. Similarly, chil-

The very young also make good companions on a Burns Craft houseboat.

dren aboard the houseboat could use free time to good advantage by learning to tie knots and splice and whip rope.

After a lengthy stay asea steer for the shore and bright lights that offer a change of pace—the landlubber's life. The stop gives opportunity for the first mate to go grocery shopping, perhaps to have her hair done and for the skipper to refuel, take on water and ice, and use the marina's shower facilities. From fellow boaters and the charts you knew what was available: out-of-town newspapers, magazines, spirits, groceries, and the like. All of which brings up the qualifications of an ideal marina—which doesn't exist: shore restrooms, snack bar, telephone, nearby shopping, store deliveries to boat, a well-protected marina, electricity, water, pump-out station, mooring bitts, short distance to town, sailor's pub, check-cashing service, free shuttle bus service, and a rent-a-car agency.

Watching a sunset, collecting shells, listening to hi-fi music may be great activities for the skipper and first mate, but teen-age crew members, male and female, are concerned about a place where the action is: a hamburger stand, pizzeria, movie theater, drug store soda fountain, and a stroll down the main drag loom large in the eyes of your junior crew; and if, as a result, a meticulous parent-planned itinerary goes by the boards—so much the better.

If the junior crew needs the support of a friend with a good voice or a troubadour with guitar, invite one along, as music and song sound better on water. En route, if you happen to meet up with another houseboat that has junior crew members of compatible ages, invite them aboard, perhaps put them up for one long leg of the journey. Maybe their parents will reciprocate, and you'll have a night's respite.

If you have not planned well, children may become restless and bored, and the proximity of each other in tight quarters can do things to the composure of all concerned. To ease the pressure of togetherness turn the children loose in a dinghy or canoe. If they are young, tie the craft to a long line and secure it at the stern of the anchored houseboat. The youngsters can paddle out the length of the line and back to the mother ship, all the while getting verbal instructions from the skipper. After the elemental skills of small boat handling—balance, rowing, and control—are mastered, the youngsters can, with untethered craft, be allowed to range farther asea, across the bay, to the lighthouse, to the marina, ashore to walk the dog, and so on.

DISCIPLINE ABOARD

Children must understand that discipline takes on a new dimension when they board a houseboat. The skipper's responsibility for the safety of his crew and craft is decreed by statutory law; no wonder his orders are crisp and immediate execution of them imperative. Even the first mate cannot intrude her opinions to create a division of authority. Long before laws were on the books, the ancient code of the sea established the skipper as master of the ship and crew, and in this modern day of houseboating, instant and unquestioning obedience to orders remains a clear-cut precept.

A child with self-control will operate rationally and rarely panic in stressful situations. The young crew member, obediently following orders, at the same time should be given enough freedom to make his own contribution, even if it be on the simplest of levels. If a child is a brat, undisciplined and disrespectful at home, houseboat experiences may not affect that behavior. On the other hand, perhaps the therapeutic values inherent in boating—activity, contact with nature, exercise, teamwork, and tradition—may serve to be inspiring teachers.

THE YOUNGEST CREW MEMBER: BABY

The houseboating couple blessed with a baby need not forgo for long their boating program. The youngest baby doesn't seem to resent being tied, strapped, or penned in its bobbing giant cradle. His welfare is assured by many modern products: canned and boxed food, various prepackaged formulas that do not require sterilization or heat, disposable diapers, and moistened towelettes, to name a few.

The feeding and sleeping schedule dictates yours until parents train and convince the baby that it is impossible to maintain a rigid schedule on a boat. Stock up on such simple-to-serve foods as formula milk, fruit juices, canned vegetables, cookies, and so forth.

A baby's skin is very sensitive to the sun. Keep exposed skin well daubed with oil or cream. Protective clothing can include one-piece suits, hat, and a sweater for evening coolness.

To control the range of baby's crawling ventures, such devices as the harness, backpack, and playpen work well. The harness can be the mountain-climber type, with a length of safety line and snap. Hooks or eyes can be placed at various strategic parts of the boat, to which the harness line can be clipped. The line can be shortened to keep the baby safe from dangerous areas or lengthened to allow for cabin floor inspection and on-deck sightseeing.

The backpack with rigid aluminum frame is ideal for supporting and carrying the baby; it can be placed upright almost anywhere on the boat where there's activity. The upright position of the pack, not unlike the Indian baby packboard, enables the baby to make observations in a natural upright position.

A folding playpen with large unbreakable toys that are familiar from home helps the baby to accept being aboard a houseboat. The playpen should be properly padded for protection against rolling seas and shaded from too much sun. Give the confined baby as much attention as possible, for companionship as well as for checking on his comfort and safety.

Before embarking on a cruise with a baby, check with the doctor and/or experienced parents for such matters as diet, sun exposure, insect repellents, bathing, and any other individual questions or concerns.

THE FAMILY DOG GOES TOO

There's no reason to farm out the family dog to a kennel when the group goes houseboating for a day or weekend trip. A dog is best conditioned to a boat by visits while the craft is docked and being worked on. Adaptation is advanced when the dog stands on a rolling deck, adjusts to the confined quarters, and experiences the sights, sounds, and odors of waterfront activity. The skipper helps by conferring with the dog's veterinarian regarding advice on food, water, elimination, and tranquilization. In general, small dogs present fewer problems than do large dogs. They shed less hair, eat less, are more agile, require less space, and don't mess as much.

When underway tie the dog on deck with a chain short enough to keep him from jumping or falling overboard. Keep the dog's quarters consistent. The aft deck is ideal as it can easily be cleaned in emergencies. A dog that has been paper-trained offers fewer problems.

The houseboat dog, besides offering companionship, is a sentry too. In periods of the crew's absence from the boat, the dog will protect it, as he does the land-based home. On the other hand, never leave the dog in an unventilated, confined area where an overhead sun can overheat the room. Provide ample water and food if the stay will be long.

The dog falling overboard is in little danger of drowning, as he will instinctively swim. A dip net with long handle is best to scoop up the floating pet, after which he will shake his coat of fur, showering the deck. If a net is unavailable, or gotten too late, the dog will usually decide to swim to shore, where you may have a difficult time hunting him down.

The dog's food needs offer few problems, as modern nutrition and packaging know-how provide the dog owner with convenient-to-serve dog foods that are properly balanced and nutritious; they come in premeasured cellophane packets that can easily be disposed of. There are no messy cans to accumulate, and no refrigeration is necessary.

Having a dog aboard is good insurance against a skipper who cruises too long and makes the children restless and cranky. "Must walk the dog!" gives a good excuse for the crew to get in some welcome leg-stretching exercise, discover woods, engage in beachcombing, and meet other dog walkers too.

When stopping at a marina always leash your dog; keep him from slobbering over visitors, barking unnecessarily, and begging for food. Keep in mind some people dislike dogs.

Many skippers and first mates would not think of going asea without their pet dog. Some seagoing dogs actually develop sea legs, take over the bow rail, enjoy the spray in their face, and with a wildly wagging tail indicate that they thoroughly enjoy the houseboating experience.

So much for the sea-adjusted dog. There are many disadvantages in having a dog aboard on any cruise beyond the very short trip. The decision to take the family dog houseboating should be weighed very carefully before giving in to children's pleas. After all, the skipper and first mate will wind up with all the responsibilities.

The dog is not a natural sailor, and many suffer from seasickness. A sick pup may hold up a trip while a veterinarian is hunted up to administer to him. Many nuisance, mischief, and incompatibility factors probably make it inadvisable to take a dog along, doubly so if the cruise is long. He resents confinement, the lack of exercise, and the unstable footing. Those insisting on taking a dog aboard should further be prepared to face the problems of shedding hair and having elimination and vomiting accidents on the deck.

In addition, the dog may cause an extreme inconvenience to all crew members that will obviate against a planned program, and a pleasant experience. Perhaps the dog's well-being is best assured by leaving him ashore, but then, skippers and mates and crews and dogs differ, and they may not see it that way at all. It's your boat and your dog; only you can judge what's best for all.

Retirees have their own interesting life-style; these two couples leave their Chris-Craft to enjoy shore lunch.

HOUSEBOATING IN RETIREMENT

When houseboating arrives, eventually and surely, full-blown and widely embraced, you can thank oldsters, who in their retirement had the courage to use the houseboat on arduous trips stateside and in foreign countries.

The retiree has discovered an interesting life-style, spending the summers plying northern waters, then like migratory birds heading south for the cold months to Florida waters, the Caribbean Sea, Gulf of Mexico, or Southern California.

These senior citizens realize that retirement can be an adventure, truly the "salad days" of life. They have chosen the houseboat over the very expensive waterfront residence and the mobile home that is situated too far from the center-of-town conveniences. Unlike their interesting water-borne home, the mobile home or trailer is strapped down to cement blocks; it is *im*mobile and rests in a monotonous grid pattern of metal rectangles. And compared to other pleasure craft, the houseboat purchase gives good value for the investment. In order to duplicate the cabin dimensions and accommodations in a conventional power cruiser, the retiree would have to buy at least twice as big a boat and invest more than double the money.

More Benefits. Retirement income, after the original boat purchase, goes a lot further than when living ashore. The live-in houseboat offers a practical, pleasant, and economical craft which serves as a home, as transportation, and as a recreation outlet. Houseboat living offers, too, a respite from the growing complexity of retired life.

Couples soon realize that there's no need to continue the pattern of life that once shackled them. Many of the shore-living expenses are eliminated: rent, constant upkeep and maintenance, taxes, utility bills, clothes requirements, and the upkeep of an automobile. Local food sources such as fish, clams, lobster, shrimp, fruits and vegetables can often be gotten "fresh" as all of these products abound in houseboating areas.

Skippering the houseboat by the husband and crewing by the wife calls for active participation, with just enough activity to bring a zestful edge to ample and well-deserved freedom. As to the travel range of your retirement craft, it's as wide, and remote, and interesting as you wish to make it. The lakes, rivers, canals of Canada, the oceans, Great Lakes, Gulf of Mexico, and tidewaters of the United States are there as

Effective service is offered at Stan Wytrwal Marina at Clinton, Iowa, including houseboat rentals, water, and power.

the spirit dictates for cruising, roaming, and anchoring. There's no great concern for schedule, weather, or tomorrow.

Marina Stops. Marinas and docks along the way serve the retired houseboater in many ways: dockage for the night or for lengthy stays, fuel and other boat needs, advice on routes, and answers to the dozens of questions that always crop up. Modern marinas also provide rest rooms, showers, lounge, boat security, and other services, the costs of which are comparable to those of highway trailer camps.

Docking at most marinas will be approximately $100 a month, including water, electricity, and garbage collection. Once berthed you plug in your hook-up, and all the appliances become operative; you have the services of stove, toaster, refrigerator, television set, vacuum cleaner, and air conditioner. Marinas are generally located in active sections of towns or resort areas and are within easy walking distance to shops, restaurants, churches, library, and art gallery.

Docked in your slip you'll find privacy for relaxation and for personal projects, and always there's the option to move to greener waters. Day trips can be enjoyed, simply by hauling up the anchor and heading to another locale to fish, picnic, or visit friends. If you're permanently located, be prepared for visits from friends, family, and grandchildren, who will enjoy the boat and the cocktails, tea, or lemonade.

The houseboater can vary his schedule, and save money too, by anchoring for an extended stay in some isolated region, perhaps with a group of other boats. During the summer months especially, anchoring out is most popular, and the company of others is welcome, as you meet with active, congenial like-minded folk. Invite them aboard for an evening of camaraderie, and in the round of parties that follows, you'll be judged by your manners and the neatness of your boat, not by your bank account, reputation, or the accessories on your boat.

Local and Distant Activities. Purposeful activities to occupy a wide swath of time are always at hand. Underway, there's the task of navigation, keeping the decks and engine room shipshape, watching route buoys, and keeping an eye to weather signs.

Docking in resort areas opens up possibilities for varied experiences that range from the gustatory to the aesthetic. You may wish to alter your west coast of Florida route to include a noted restaurant, such as Papa's in Tarpon Springs, or continue up the coast to catch a glimpse of the sea cow (manatee) at Crystal River.

Fishing is a popular interest for many retired houseboaters. When fish for the table is called for, it's but a matter of trolling a line from the stern deck while underway; especially in the ocean, this simple and effortless method will capture fish for the table. In other areas, it's just a matter of locating them (with a fish finder), anchoring, baiting up, and hauling up a mess. Oysters, clams, and crabs can also be had, though with a little more effort. A lobster permit may be purchased and traps set out for this expensive delicacy.

Bird watching can develop into a hobby that will challenge the retiree for the rest of his life. The identification of water birds, the checking of rare and endangered species, observing their mating, nesting, and rearing of young are aspects of nature that too few people know about. Migration, for instance—the traveling habits of feathered creatures—represents mysteries that defy the understanding of modern scientists, as it did the cave men. By taking part in the annual Audubon bird count (the last week in December) you'll have the satisfaction of contributing to knowledge of bird populations, their increase or decrease, along with some ecosystem influences.

Retiree in Paris, France. One of the pioneers in making use of the houseboat as a permanent pad in retirement was Ney MacMinn, retired Northwestern University professor, who lived aboard a houseboat on the River Seine in Paris after retiring in 1960. His back and front yards were the tree-lined banks, sculptured bridges, and Eiffel Tower in the distance. "I've become very fond of that tower. I've seen it in the rain, the fog, and in moonlight—it is constantly changing," he said.

The professor explained getting away from it all: no doorbell, telephone, postman, car, radio, or television. Contained in his floating home were only the things he needed for peaceful escape: a huge coffee cup, smoking pipe, phonograph, cello, a pet dog, and his collection of 6,000 books that lined every wall, including the bathroom.

MacMinn purchased the 59-ton, 74-foot-long boat in Holland, and Paris officials granted him a permit to dock on the Seine next to the French, Dutch, and Italian houseboats a few blocks from the plush George V hotel. The professor neatly evaded Paris's high rents with a small investment, converting the $1,500 barge into a room, kitchen, study, two bedrooms, and bathroom. As to loneliness, the professor indicated. "I've never been lonely, I've always been happy because I'm self-sufficient. I read, I think, I listen to music, play the cello, entertain old friends, or play with the dog."

Houseboating, then, offers to the retiree a youthful outlook on life, a program of happy activity, and exercise that promotes health. The heavy tan, expertise in boat handling, and general aura of the houseboating retiree help to conceal his age, and the landlubber would be hard pressed to judge whether the skipper was 60, 70, or 80 years old.

Once convinced that the houseboat looms large in a prospective retiree's plans, the ideal way to start is to purchase a boat while still working, getting in some advanced savvy before that continuous and carefree retirement.

In essence, the retired couple oriented to the water will choose a houseboat to get away from the formal and stilted, high-density type of living, cooped up with neighbors they can't easily change if they are incompatible. With a houseboat it is easy to move, and it can be stored when the retirees decided to go land traveling to visit children, grandchildren, or old friends.

Houseboat living is quite stable in an economically unstable world, and there's some assurance that in 5 years the cost of enjoying the style now lived will not have appreciably risen. And the retiree doesn't want to get involved in buying a house that he knows will not be in accord with his income 5 years hence. Houseboat/retirement represents a great combination.

10

The Flotilla of
Houseboat Models

This informative section for the prospective houseboat buyer codifies specifications, standard and optional equipment, the power package, and the price of models currently on the market.

As is evident from preceding discussion, the range of houseboats is wide. From the boat with dual pontoons upon which is placed a simple boxy superstructure to the large, custom-crafted, luxury-studded job, and from a price of $4,850 to $67,000, there's a craft for everyone, one to suit *your* personal needs—navigation, housing, and financial.

Houseboats are manufactured in many states and in three provinces of Canada and are generally located near suitable houseboating waters. This widespread pattern of sources places a manufacturer close to home for many houseboaters. This proximity has advantages. The customer can visit a plant for complete inspection of the construction process and a possible trial run prior to a decision. Also, shipping costs will be less when you patronize a nearby company.

Zeroing in through the bewildering mass of information—hulls of fiberglass, aluminum, steel, and superstructures of wood, aluminum, and steel, standard and optional equipment, power, price, and so forth —can be a big chore and actually a lot of fun. In either buying your first houseboat or trading up, the shopping can start by studying the overview of available models listed on the following pages. Beyond that, spend a lot of time at the nearest dock or marina, the local boat show, and dealers' showrooms. Write companies for literature; read and compare models for specifications, standard equipment, power, and price; and test drive if possible to help make a judgment.

To better understand the presentation of models, some "trade" characteristics are noted:

1. Note the standard equipment of all models in a given line. They are interchangeable and you can add, or refuse, almost any feature you deem necessary or unnecessary.

2. In a line of multiple models, most of the features of a lower-priced model are automatically included in a model that is higher priced. These carry-over standard features will not be repeated for the higher-priced models.

3. Most models include obvious standard items. Galleys, for the most part, include range and oven, stainless-steel sink, and hot-cold running water. To indicate the presence of these items in the summaries below, "complete galley" shall be used. Likewise, "complete head" shall indicate a marine toilet, full-size shower, sink, and mirror; and "complete lighting system" shall indicate approved International Navigation Lights, shore power connectors, 12-volt and 120-volt systems aboard.

4. Optional equipment, being interchangeable, shall be itemized once for each company to prevent repetition from model to model.

In this day of rising costs, all manufacturers of houseboats include in their literature, "Orders accepted subject to prices prevailing at time of delivery," and "We reserve the right to make changes in models, prices, materials, and specifications at any time without notice." Thus, all prices quoted on houseboat models and options throughout this section are approximate and subject to change.

Houseboat manufacturers, in their literature, use many abbreviations; their interpretations are noted here and shall be used in the discussion of models:

cu ft	cubic feet	kw	kilowatt, a unit of electrical power
°	degrees of measurement	mph	miles per hour
′	foot (measurement)	N/A	not available
″	inch (measurement)	V	volt
gal	gallon	V-8	8 cylinders (motor)
hp	horsepower	w/	with
I/O	inboard-outboard (motor)	wt	weight

BUYER'S GUIDE

All of the following specifications, standard equipment, safety features, and performance claims are based upon material supplied by the companies whose products are listed.

■ **Aluminum Cruisers,** Inc., Standiford Field, Louisville, Kentucky 40213.
Model and specifications: Marinette 28, aluminum construction, length 28′, beam 10′5″, draft 2′, wt (single engine) 5,410 pounds,

LEFT: *Aluminum Cruisers Sea-Crest.* BELOW: *Americana Living Cruiser.* BOTTOM: *Boatel Tradewind and Cruiser*

(twin) 6,520 pounds, freeboard forward and aft 4'6" and 3', headroom 6'3", sleeps 4, sundeck 6'11", cockpit 9'9", forward deck 7'2". Power: Chrysler V-8 225 hp, or optional Twin V-8. Price: $10,920.

Standard equipment: Screened sliding windows and door, safety plate glass forward, carpeted cabin floor, insulated cabin, 25-gal water tank, 53-gal fuel tank, complete galley, head, and lighting systems.

Model: Marinette 32, aluminum, length 32'4", beam 11'6", draft 2', freeboard and aft 55" and 41", headroom 6'3", sleeps 6, sundeck 9', cockpit 10', cabin length 13', forward deck 7'8". Power: Same as above. Price: $14,645.

Standard equipment: Fire extinguishers, 5 cabin lights and all the items in the 28' model above.

Model: Sea-Crest 41, aluminum construction, length 41', beam 13'6", freeboard forward and aft 44" and 37", sleeps 6 or more. Power: Chrysler V-8 Twin 225 hp. Price: $26,3000.

Standard equipment: Many deluxe features.

Optional equipment (for all models): Electric bilge pump $60, searchlight $45, anchor and chocks $45, boarding ladder $70, flying bridge with dual controls $1,900, stereo with 4 speakers $250, docking lights (pair) $115, bow rail $185, depth sounder $175, automatic generating plant 110-V $1,875, drapes, rods, fasteners $350, Danforth anchor $55, air conditioner $695, transom platform with boarding step and gate opening $425, engine hour meter $35, wet bar $150, and many others.

■ **Americana Living Cruisers** (formerly Royal Craft Marine), 220 Columbia Title Bldg., Topeka, Kansas 66612.

Models: Custom-made Living Cruisers are in the 50' or longer class with the accent on spacious living and entertaining. Some floor plans and exterior designs are suggested but the company's general objective is to give the luxury boat buyer the opportunity to specify the size, design, floor plan, furnishings, and decor that fit the desires of the buyer and his family or company.

A prototype is offered which gives a point of beginning to assist people in designing their own boat, building into it their own pet ideas and tastes to evolve a very personal craft.

Architects, engineers, industrial designers, and boat owners advised on what they thought should be included in an ideal houseboat. The Living Cruiser prototype is built with catamaran hulls in which everything, except the sundeck, is on one level offering a huge living area. By night the forward salon and dinette are converted into private staterooms (to sleep 6) by means of wooden folding doors.

Price: The cost of models 50' or longer with a beam of 14' to 16' will range from $75,000 upward.

■ **Boatel Co. Inc.,** 24 Walnut St., Mora, Minnesota 55051.

Model and specifications: Tradewind 37, fiberglass hull, length 37', beam 12', draft 26", freeboard forward 40", aft 31", headroom 6'11", cabin 9' x 22', wt 13,000 pounds, sleeps 8. Power: 235-hp I/O Mer-Cruiser. Price: $17,681 (with other power options up to $20,925).

Standard equipment: Interior teak wood grain vinyl paneling, teak doors and trim, shag carpeting, 2 convertible sofas in 3 color choices, complete galley, head, and lighting systems, 2 cedar-lined wardrobe lockers, bilge pump and blower, fuel tank 68 gal, water tank 45 gal, teak handrails, 5-chain protected gates, 4 cleats, 1 mooring bitt.

Model: Islander 47, fiberglass hull, length 47', beam 13', draft 28", forward freeboard 54", aft 41", headroom 5'9", (stateroom) 6'6" (cabin), sleeps 10, cabin 10'6" x 32', wt 21,000 pounds. Power: Twin 225-hp I/O Chrysler engines. Price: $37,850 (with other power options, up to $54,990).

Standard equipment: Teak wood grain paneling, teak cabinet and drawer fronts, shag carpeting, 2 sofas, convertible cocktail and dining table, padded control console, liquor cabinet, complete galley, head, and lighting systems, tachometer, oil pressure, fuel, temperature gauges, etc.

Optional equipment: Air conditioner $1,550 to $2,755, bottle gas tank $87, fume detector $260, ice maker $500, boarding ladder $70, drapes $480, wall-mounted heater $110, holding tank 20 gal $230, brass fittings $210, power steering $385, flying bridge $2,400, storage cradle $325, etc.

■ **Burns Craft**, 2940 E. Avalon, Muscle Shoals, Alabama 35660.

Models are 5 in number and designated as Burns Craft 32', 35', 43', 45', and 50'. The 32', 43', and 50' models are here summarized.

Model: Burns Craft 32, all fiberglass-reinforced construction, length 32', beam 12', freeboard 42", walkways 18", draft 16", cabin 21' x 9', complete galley, head, and lighting systems, water capacity 55 gal, fuel 60 gal, wt 11,000 pounds, etc. Power: 225-hp I/O Chrysler. Price: $11,994.

Standard equipment: All-white polyester gel coat finish, painted steel handrails and sundeck ladder, anodized aluminum windows, vinyl floor covering, hanging locker, convertible L-shape lounge in wheelhouse, paneling ¼" throughout, complete head, galley, and lighting systems.

Model: Burns Craft 43, overall length 43', beam 12', draft 16", freeboard forward 49", aft 40", cabin 28'5" x 9', headroom 7', forward deck 8'7", aft deck 5,9", wt 18,000, water capacity 55 gal, fuel capacity 150 gal. Power: Twin 225-hp I/O Chrysler. Price: $22,440.

Standard equipment: In addition to the above, custom instrument panel, twin gas tanks, 12-V bilge blower, hot water heater, 6 dockside cleats, dockside power inlet with 50' cord, etc.

Burns Craft

Carri-Craft Cruis-Ader

Model: Burns Craft 50, fiberglass construction, length 50', beam 15', walkways 18", freeboard forward 45", aft 44", draft 33", cabin 34'8" x 10'8", forward deck 7'7", aft deck 6'5", sundeck length 17', water capacity 90 gal, fuel capacity 200 gal. Power: Twin 225-hp V-8 Chrysler. Price: $31,670.

Standard equipment: Anchor light, engine ventilating system, overhead cabinets in galley and stateroom, insulated roof, chart area in console, stainless steel rails, paneling throughout. See above models for more standard features.

Optional equipment: For all models, flying bridge, air conditioner, heater, engine options, etc. Prices available upon request.

■ **Carri-Craft Inc.,** 328 Ripon Road, Berlin, Wisconsin 54923.

Model and specifications: Cruis-Ader 45, reinforced fiberglass hull, length 45', beam 14', draft 3'6", freeboard forward 6', aft 5', height from waterline 12'6", headroom 6'4", water capacity 110 gal, fuel capacity 220 gal. Power: Twin 215-hp V-8 MerCruiser. Price: $45,000.

Standard equipment: Complete lighting system, galley, and head with holding tank, 34-pound anchor with chocks, 3 batteries, 3 bilge blowers, breakers on all circuits, binnacle box with dual instruments, compass, 3 windshield wipers, mast with anchor light, 8" spotlight, generator, lighted closets, built-in cabinets in galley, tinted glass windows, 3 heaters, etc.

Model: Cruis-Ader 57, fiberglass, length 57', beam 14', draft 3'6", freeboard forward 6', aft 5', height from waterline 12'6", headroom 6'4", water capacity 110 gal, fuel capacity 330 gal. Power: Twin 270-hp V-8 MerCruiser. Price: $57,000.

Standard equipment: Same as the 45' model plus 14-cu-ft refrigerator with automatic ice maker, mattresses and box springs, 2 heads with holding tanks, separate tub/shower areas, and other features.

Optional equipment: Air conditioning $712 to $1,372, anchoring windlass (500 pounds) vertical capstan $1,075, flying bridge with controls and instruments $3,800, ring buoy w/hangers $50, fenders 10" x 26" round $35, stern deck conversion for sport fishing $2,500, Diesel engine option 160-hp Perkins 1.5:1 V-drive $10,826, freight rail packing and loading $375, and various hardware parts, props, rails, mooring lines.

LEFT: *Chris-Craft Aqua-Home*. BELOW: *Georgian*

■ **Chris-Craft Industries Inc.**, Box 860, Pompano Beach, Florida 33061. Also, 600 Madison Ave., New York, New York 10022.

Model and specifications: Aqua-Home 34, maintenance free fiberglass construction, length 34', beam 12'10", draft 36½", freeboard forward 31", sleeps 6, fuel capacity 125 gal, water capacity 80 gal. Power: Twin 200-hp V-Drive Chris-Craft. Price $19,425.

Standard equipment: Complete galley with rotisserie, anchor light, bilge blower, complete lighting system and 50' cord with adaptor and plug, 2 fire extinguishers, hull drain plug, fog bell, mahogany handrails with gates, 6 life preservers, electric horn, insulated cabin and deckhouse roof, sliding door and windows (anodized aluminum) with screens, etc.

Model: Aqua-Home 46, fiberglass construction, length 46', beam 15', draft 29½", freeboard forward 44", sleeps 8 to 10, water capacity 100 gal, fuel capacity 240 gal, shipping height (with cradle) 11'10", weight 16,666 pounds. Power: Twin 235-hp V-Drive Chris-Craft. Price: $29,000.

Standard equipment: In addition to most features above, the following: galley includes double stainless steel sink w/spray rinse, interior carpeting and drapery, convertible lounge, stainless steel ladder w/teak treads, lighting system with circuit breaker fusing, drop leaf table, bedspread, 3 fire extinguishers, 8 life preservers, automatic bilge pump, etc.

Optional equipment: Extra pair of props $271, generator (6.5-kw Onan) $2,765, additional dockside wiring $535, Danforth anchor 22# w/shackle $59, anchor line 150' of ⅝" nylon w/thimble $44, dual controls and instruments on sundeck $2,290, extra cleats and spring line (pair) $29, drapes throughout cabins installed with valances $613, air conditioner $1,890, marine head systems $189 to $621, compass $77, depth sounder $250, command bridge w/dual controls etc. $3,986, wall-type heater $146, shipping cradle $228, and such items as stereo tape player, searchlight, monomatic toilet system, compass, etc.

■ **Georgian Steel Boats Ltd.,** 310 Arvin Ave., Stoney Creek, Ontario, Canada.

Model and specifications: Georgian 33, a steel boat protected with a "seallife" process, a zinc-rich compound fusing with an epoxy binder directly to the hull through electrochemical action. Length 32'7", beam 12', draft 30", height 9'7", wt 9,700 pounds, sleeps 6. Power: Single 225-hp OMC stern drive. Price: $17,600.

Standard equipment: Soundproofed hull interior, hot and cold water pressure system, stern swim ladder, complete galley, head, and lighting systems, window screens, wall-to-wall carpeting, fully insulated cabin, water capacity 60 gal, fuel 45 gal, walk-around side decks and railing, convertible dinette and settee, etc.

Model: Georgian 38, steel hull as above, length 37'7", beam 12', draft 30", height 9'7", wt 11,500 pounds, sleeps 6. Power: Twin 165-hp OMC stern drive. Price: $23,975.
Standard equipment: Same as above.

Model: Georgian 43, steel hull as above, length 42'7", beam 12', draft 32", height 9'7", wt 12,700 pounds, sleeps 8. Power: Twin 225-hp OMC stern drive. Price: $27,200.
Standard equipment: Same as Georgian 33' model.
Optional equipment: Patio-type flight deck $1,240, flying bridge $2,220, captains swivel seat $49, draperies $344, water purifier $97, front safety glass $152, power steering $376, depth sounder $220, carpet underpad $84, and others.

■ **Harbor House Corp.,** Highway 19, Wakarusa, Indiana 46573.
Models and specifications: The Harbor House models are offered in 6 different floor plans, aluminum construction, tri-hull design, and are sold directly from factory to customer. All models include the following specifications: length 46', beam 13'6", draft forward and aft 10" and

Harbor House

14", freeboard forward 48", aft 41", cabin size 10'6" x 30', main salon headroom 6'6", water capacity 100 gal, fuel 205 gal, holding tank 100 gal, sleeps 6 to 10, approximate mph 34, hydraulic steering. Power: Twin 225-hp MerCruisers with closed cooling system. Price: averages about $1,000 a foot, including make-ready and shakedown.

Standard features: Exterior: Cabin construction 090 marine aluminum alloy, hull 187 welded marine aluminum alloy, sliding windows and screens w/latches, tinted safety glass, anchor 35 pound w/chocks and 100' line, Marinium mooring bitts and 9" cleats, outdoor carpeting on decks, boathook w/ brackets, windshield wiper, running lights, 52" flagmast with anchor light, automatic bilge pumps, and command bridge with seat.

Electrical, gas, and plumbing systems: Gas furnace w/ thermostat, blower and pilot lighting, underfloor heating system, air conditioner, shore power hookup w/2 50' cords, interior and exterior light outlets, 100-gal holding tank, pressurized water system 8 gal, gas water heater, 7.5-kw generator, etc.

Interior: Pile shag carpeting, color-keyed interiors, drapes and linings, foam insulation in ceiling, floor, and walls, bar w/electric refrigerator, stereo tape/AM-FM, radio system w/4 speakers and remote control in master stateroom, magic-bed w/Sealy posturepedic mattresses, built-in vacuum cleaner, pilot's console w/full engine instrumentation, mounted compass, etc.

Galley: Magic Chef 4-burner range and oven w/glass door and light, 8-cu-ft gas/electric refrigerator w/freezer, range exhaust hood and light, double stainless steel sink, and convertible dinette w/tufted back and 5" cushions.

Head: Full-size tub and shower, sliding shower door, clothes hamper, linen closet, privacy door w/lock, plastic laminated lavatory top, vinyl wall coverings, and large mirror.

Safety features: Rounded corners on doors, drawers, and cabinets, 4 fire extinguishers, fire-retardent foam flotation, circuit breakers, 3 banks of batteries w/selector switch, shut-off valves on gas appliances and gasoline lines, tinted glass, fire-retardant drapes and linings, sealed combustion furnace, ventilated and trapped plumbing system, and many more.

Optional equipment: Engine options $400 to $2,500, deluxe electrical package $400, deluxe interior package $1,200, Bimini top $150, davits $300, pilot chair $50, swim platform w/ladder $500, air conditioning $500 to $2,850, gas furnace w/floor ducts, Frigidaire $50 to $700, washer & dryer $575.

■ **Holiday Mansion**, 615 E. Pacific, Salina, Kansas 67401.
Model and specifications: Wanderer II, pontoon boat with 12 water-tight bulkheads, length 33', beam, 10', cabin 10' x 16', wt 6,200 pounds,

Holiday Mansion-Crown Royal

load capacity 4,500 pounds, sleeps 6. Power: Suggested 50- to 80-hp outboard motor (not included). Price: $8,245.

Standard equipment: Complete head, galley, and lighting systems, cable steering, convertible dinette seats (to sleeping), inlaid linoleum, fiberglass deck planking, sundeck, sliding glass windows, screened door, etc.

Model: Crown Royal 51, steel and fiberglass construction, catamaran hull, length 51'3¼" beam 13'4½", freeboard forward 4'8", aft 2'10", draft 18", cabin size 30'1" x 11'8½", sleeps 6 to 9. Power: Twin 130-hp I/O Chrysler Volvos standard. Price $22,995.

Standard equipment: Private bedroom conversion, living-room carpeting, 3 high-backed padded bad stools, 2 swivel rocker occasional chairs, cigarette lighter and map light, twin control panels, 24" spoked wood helmsman wheel, complete lighting system, galley with 20-gal electric water heater, 9 overhead cabinets, 5 storage drawers, full-length wardrobes, complete head with medicine cabinet, water system hot and cold, 60-gal capacity, tinted glass, circuit breakers, nonslip planking on decks, natural wood paneling, full insulation, 4 mooring cleats, etc.

Model: 5th Avenue was designed primarily for boat rental operators with their inexperienced clientele in mind. For maximum long life deck sides are replaceable with finished 4" x 4". The bow is reinforced from underside, and the hull is inset 3" on each side to protect the cabin walls. Rails meet new B.I.A. standards of withstanding a tension pull of 300 pounds from any direction. Natural wood paneling ¼" resists scratches that are easily covered or mended.

Specifications: Pontoon length 41', beam 10', cabin 9' x 24', draft 12", wt 8,900 pounds, load capacity 4,100 pounds, sleeps 8 to 10. Power: 50- to 110-hp outboard motor (not included). Price: $9,882.

Two other models, the Penthouse 39' priced at $8,245, and the Executive 47' priced at $13,987 (plus power plant), are also popular as rental units.

Optional equipment for all models: Flying bridge w/access ladder, steering controls, instruments, $2,995, electric refrigerator with ice maker $525, electric range w/oven $185, 6.5-kw generator $1,995, air conditioner $525, automatic bilge pump $87, depth finder $225, Mon-o-Matic head $245, drapes $295. Gasoline engine options $725 to $995, Diesels $3,800 and $5,200.

■ **Kayot Marine Division,** 500 Industrial Road North, Mankato Minnesota 56001.

Model and specifications: Caprice 30, steel, V-bottom pontoons, length 30', beam 10', draft 15", sleeps 4, cabin 9'6" x 14', headroom 76", decks, forward 10' x 8', aft 10' x 6', sundeck 9'6" x 14', wt 6,300 pounds. Power: outboard motor of your choice, long-shaft 50-to 80-hp is suggested (not included in price). Price $7,250. An aluminum model is available for $8,125.

Standard equipment: Complete galley, head, and lighting systems, electric horn, sundeck rails, dinette-bed conversion, water capacity 30 gal, holding tank 30 gal w/dockside discharge, vinyl cabin flooring, safety

Kayot Royal Capri and Caprice

glass w/screens in doors and windows, helmstand, aluminum siding, insulated fiberglass sidewalls, nonskid deck, etc.

Model: Royal Capri III, steel construction, V-bottom pontoons, length 40', beam 12', draft 15", sleeps 9, cabin 9'6" x 14', headroom 76", forward deck 12' x 10', aft deck 12' x 6', sundeck 9'6" x 22', wt 10,450 pounds. Power: outboard motor as above. Price: $11,990.

Standard equipment: Most of the above items, complete galley, head, and lighting systems, electric horn, bell, 12-V water heater, L-shape dinette w/vinyl upholstery, 4" polyfoam cushions, double bed w/overhead storage, folding privacy curtain, drapes, screens, 6 mooring cleats, prewired for stereo, etc.

Optional equipment: Fuel tank 28 gal $75, Monomatic head $285, gas heater $120, LP gas level indicator $20, spotlight w/remote control, boarding ladder $30, etc.

■ **Kings Craft,** Box 2306, Florence, Alabama 35630.

Model and specifications: Home Cruiser 35, aluminum construction, length 35', beam 12', draft 30", wt 8,000 pounds, freeboard forward 38", aft 37", hull bottom and sides $\frac{3}{16}$" and $\frac{1}{8}$" aluminum, headroom 6'6", cabin 9' x 23'6", sleeps 6, forward deck 7' x 12', aft deck 12' x 4'6", sundeck 8' x 13', water capacity 125 gal, fuel 90 gal. Power: Single 215-hp engine (capable of 30 mph) and Twin 215-hp engine (capable of 36 mph). Price $16,995 with single engine, $20,625 with twin engines.

Standard equipment: Electric bilge blower and pump, mast with anchor light, rub molding, 6 cleats, anchor, pressure hot water system, 6" ship's bell, complete lighting system w/dockside hookup connectors, 2 fire extinguishers, convertible dinette, pilothouse and aft cabins into sleeping berths, reversible cushions, walnut marine paneling, shag or plush-pile carpeting, laminated plastic top counters, cabinets, and dinette table, custom galley and a complete head, liquor storage cabinet, collision bulkhead, safety glass windows w/screens, sliding glass doors, 360° pilothouse vision.

Kings Craft Home Cruiser

Model: Home Cruiser 40, aluminum, length 40', beam 12', draft 31", wt 10,500 pounds, freeboard forward 40", aft 35", hull bottom and sides ³⁄₁₆" and ³⁄₈" aluminum, headroom 6'6", cabin 9' x 28'6", sleeps 8, forward deck 7' x 12', aft 12' x 4'6", sundeck 15'6" x 9', water capacity 150 gal, fuel 180 gal. Power: Single 225-hp engine (capable of 25 mph) and Twin 225-hp engine (capable of 32 mph). Price: $21,350 with single engine, $25,175 with twin engines.

Standard equipment: In addition to the features listed for the 35' model the following: electric horn, 12-cu-ft refrigerator, and 8 fire extinguishers.

Model: Home Cruiser 44, aluminum, length 44', beam 15', draft 32", wt 14,000 pounds, freeboard forward 40", aft 36", hull bottom and sides ³⁄₁₆" and ³⁄₈" aluminum, headroom 6'6", cabin 40'6" x 12', sleeps 10, forward deck 15' x 9', aft deck 15' x 5'6", sundeck 23' x 12', water capacity 200 gal, fuel 180 gal. Power: Twin 225-hp engine (capable of 30 mph). Price: $32,350.

Standard equipment: In addition to the features listed above, the following: Magnesium anodes on hull and propeller units, water heater, custom drapes installed, Perko searchlight, 8-track tape system w/4 speakers, upholstered easy chair, stern boarding ladder, folding doors, wet bar, 1" marine aluminum rails, chrome gates for rail openings.

Model: Home Cruiser 55, aluminum, length 55', beam 15', draft 34", wt 18,500 pounds, freeboard forward 42", aft 38", hull bottom and sides ³⁄₁₆" and ⅛" aluminum, headroom 6'6", cabin 40'6" x 12', sleeps 10, forward deck 15' x 9', aft deck 15' x 5'6", sundeck 23' x 12', water capacity 250 gal, fuel 180 gal. Power: Twin 225-hp engine (capable of 28 mph). Price: $48,000.

Standard equipment: In addition to the features above, the following: Danforth White compass, 2 electric bilge pumps, 7.5-kw generator w/2 transfer switches, refrigerator w/ice maker, 110-V system w/circuit breaker, electromagnetic head, engine mufflers, docking lights, central heating/cooling systems, windshield wipers, ensign socket w/staff, 4 fire extinguishers, master stateroom w/twin or queen-size bed, and Drexel hi-lo table.

Optional equipment: Please note that several options are included as standard in the 44′ and 55′ models. Wet bar $60, dual trumpet horn $175, electric head w/chlorinator $375, Monomatic head $430, holding tank 25 gal $175, Perko searchlight (200,000 candlepower) $105, captain's chair $90, Danforth White compass $70, extra fire extinguisher $21, draperies $395, davits (400 pounds) $265, stereo system 4-8 track w/4 speakers $225, air conditioner $675, command bridge w/canvas $2,150, Bimini top-bridge $225, cigarette lighter and chart light combination $24, depth sounder $185, mooring bit 4″ $24, central vacuum system $295, intercom system $70, astroturf on exterior decks $250, factory launch and make-ready $175 to $350.

■ **Lazy-Days Manufacturing Co. Inc.,** Holiday Rd., Buford, Georgia 30518.

Model and specifications: Sportsman 50, aluminum, length 50′2″, beam 14′6″, draft 18″, freeboard forward 35″, aft 24″, cabin 35′ x 11′8″, forward deck 9′ long, aft deck 6′ long, depth of hull deck to chine 30″, keel 6″, walkway width 17″, overall height 9′ (w/command bridge 12′4″), headroom 6′6″, sleeps 6 or more, water capacity 84 gal, fuel 84 gal. Power: Several engine options available. Price: $36,967.

Standard equipment: The equipment and furnishings listed here are standard for all Lazy-Days houseboats: Navigation lights, electric horn, permanent front awning, 12-V automatic fresh water pump, 115-V hot-water heater, complete lighting system, 6 ceiling lights w/12-V and

Lazy Days Custom 61

115-V bulbs, reading lights over each bed, 12-V bilge blower, polarity indicator, complete galley w/rotisserie, drapes w/rods and hardware for all doors and windows, optional floor plans, complete head w/marble lavatory, medicine chest, vinyl tile floors, screens on all windows and sliding glass door, railing on cabin roof and around decks 20", mahogany marine-type steering wheel.

Model: Sportsman 56, offered with all of the above specifications, except that the overall length is 56'2", cabin is 40'8" long, and sleeping is for 8 or more.

Standard equipment: Additional equipment to the above includes guest stateroom with 54" x 74" bed, 3 large drawers under bed, 115-V reading light over bed, head includes marine toilet, medicine cabinet, chrome-plated soap dish, toothbrush, glass, and paper holder, stainless-steel lavatory with storage under. Power: Several engine options available. Price: $35,842.

Model: Custom 55, aluminum, length 35'6", beam 14'6", draft 16", freeboard forward 75", aft 33", forward deck 12'10" long, aft deck 7'6" long, cabin 35'2" x 18'8", depth of hull deck to chine 43", keel 6", walkway width 17", overall height 9'9" (w/command bridge 13'1"), sleeps 6 and more, water capacity 120 gal, fuel 120 gal. Power: Engine options available. Price: $36,942.

Standard equipment: Same as for the model above.

Model: Custom 61 is offered with all the above specifications and standard equipment, except that the overall length is 61', length of cabin is 12'10", sleeping is for 8 or more. Price: $44,997.

Optional equipment: Air conditioner $495 and $595, anchor 10-pound $20 and 36-pound $54, anchor windlass $220, bar w/ice maker, sink, water, storage closet with lock, glass racks, and bottle holder $640, battery chargers for 3 separate batteries, bridge command w/dual steering, shift, throttle and dual instruments $3,400, carpeting $495 to $564, davits (500-pound capacity) $195, depth sounder $165 to $380, flag pole $38, fume detector $165, air horn $148, radiotelephone $496, ship's wheel 32" $92, and others.

■ **Maurell Products Inc.,** 2711 South M-52, Owosso, Michigan 48867.

Model and specifications: Crest 3508, pontoon houseboat w/22"-dia. aluminum pontoons w/canoe-type nose cones, length 35', beam 8', cabin 8' x 17', forward, aft, and sundecks, gaucho and single bunks sleeps 4 to 6, closet, wt 2,900 pounds, load capacity 4,000 pounds. Power: Supply your own outboard motor in the suggested range 25 to 60 hp. Price: $5,275.

Standard equipment: Complete galley, head w/holding tank, and lighting system, jalousie glass door and screen, water tank, cabin of marine aluminum construction w/insulated walls.

Model: Crest 3510, aluminum pontoons 26"-dia. x 35' long, beam 10', cabin 17' x 10', forward, aft, and sundecks, sleeps 4 to 6, wt 3,700 pounds, load capacity 5,000 pounds. Power: Recommended is a long-shaft 25- to 60-hp outboard. Price: $6,395.

Standard equipment: Same as the above model.

Optional equipment: Swivel bucket seat $76, combination 12- and 110-V light $10 each, 10,000 Btu furnace $96, oven and 3-burner range $90, wall-mounted heating and air conditioning $325, double gas tanks $45, double sink $24, water tank 55 gal $45, electric water pump $50, shower unit $95, etc.

■ **MonArk Boat Co.,** P.O. Box 210, Monticello, Arkansas 71655.

The company no longer builds a production model houseboat. The offered houseboats are completely customized and built for the man who wants to have a say in the design and construction. As a result the boats range from $50,000 to $200,000 each.

A popular model is the Executive, of aluminum construction, 53' length, 13' beam, 48" fore freeboard, 42" aft, 30" draft, which sleeps 6, and is powered by an I/O 250-hp engine, and sells in the $50,000s.

■ **Maxa Industries Inc.,** 1603 E. Florida St., Springfield, Missouri 65903.

Model and specifications: Maxa-Craft, steel hull, length 32', beam 10', walkways 12", cabin 18' x 18', forward deck 8' x 10', sun deck 10'9" x 8', freeboard forward and aft 36" and 24", transom 10-gauge welded steel, cabin sides prefinished aluminum bonded to exterior plywood, sleeps 6, water capacity 30 gal. Power and price: N/A.

Standard equipment: Aluminum windows w/screens, sundeck railings, 4 mooring cleats, approved lighting system, deep center keel, vinyl floor covering throughout, ample storage space and hanging closet, hardwood paneling, 360° pilothouse, 18" captain's wheel, complete galley and head.

Optional equipment: N/A.

Maxa-Craft

Nauta-Line

■ **Nauta-Line Inc.**, 1 Nauta-Line Dr., Hendersonville, Tennessee 37075.

Model and specifications: Nauta-line 34, fiberglass hull, length 34', beam 11'10", keel 6", draft 1'9", freeboard forward and aft 2'8" and 2'2", transom height from waterline and width 2'6" and 11'8", walkways 1'6", cabin 21'6" x 9'2", headroom 6'6", forward deck 5', aft deck 6', sun deck 9'9". Fuel capacity 72 gal, water capacity 50 gal, windows and door w/safety glass, shag carpeting, wt 14,000 pounds, sleeps 8. Power: Single 225-hp MerCruiser I/O w/power trim and power steering. Other engine options are offered $362 to $3,926. Price: Base $16,964.

Standard equipment: Walnut wood paneling, safety rails, center point steering, choice of decor, complete lighting system w/110-V Hubbell dockside connection, laminated dinette table top and counter, 22" wheel, control panel, gauges: gas, water, temperature, oil pressure, hour meter, raised pilothouse, tie cleats and mooring bit, electric bilge pump, ship's bell, horn, 8 life jackets, 3 fire extinguishers, marine distress kit, etc.

Model: Nauta-Line 43, fiberglass hull, length 43', beam 13'11", draft 1'10", freeboard forward and aft 3'2" and 2'4", transom height from waterline and width 2'7" and 11'11", walkways 1'8", cabin 28'6" x 10'6", headroom 6'6", fuel capacity 210 gal, water capacity 100 gal, windows and door w/safety glass, shag carpeting, sleeps 10. Power: Twin 225-hp MerCruiser I/O w/power trim and power steering. Engine options as above. Price: Base $28,740.

Standard equipment: In addition to most of the above, the following: Lounge and dinette bed conversions, 4 storage lockers, 12-V lights (4), 110-V lights (2), combination 12-V and 110-V lights (7), 11 outlets, upright refrigerator, vinyl-covered dinette wall, complete galley, head, and lighting systems, all gauges as in 34' model, slider panel for access to controls and wiring, fused circuits, sundeck carpeting, 6 tie cleats, 1 mooring bit, water capacity 50 gal (2), bilge pumps, windshield wiper, 8 life jackets, 4 fire extinguishers, safety glass, distress kit, etc.

Optional equipment: Custom drapes $586, privacy door aft $290, 40-gal holding tank $175, electric wall heater $108, air conditioner $776, 6.5-kw generator $2,372, depth finder $163, 2 docking lights $96, extra fuel tank $232, electric head and chlorinator $527, fume detector $242, occasional chair for pilothouse $102, searchlight $91, compass $57, stereo 8 track w/FM radio and 4 speakers $279, wet bar in pilothouse $156, fly-bridge w/instrumentation and hydraulic steering $2,718, shipping cradle $531, etc.

■ **Pacemaker Corp.,** P.O. Box 337, Egg Harbor City, New Jersey 08216.

Model and specifications: Drift-R-Cruz 35, fiberglass construction, length 35'2", beam 12', freeboard forward and aft 39" and 38", draft 30', headroom 6'6", fuel capacity 50 gal, water capacity 100 gal, approx. wt w/single engine 14,000 pounds, sleeps 6. Power options and prices: Twin 220-hp Crusader inboard $19,695, Twin 270-hp Crusader inboard $20,495, and Twin Osco Ford Diesel inboard $22,295.

Standard equipment: Anchor light, bell and bracket, bilge pump and blowers, engine alarm systems, 3 fire extinguishers, complete galley, head, and lighting systems, 12-gal hot water tank-heater, horn, ladders, safety glass windshield, control panel w/breaker switches, etc.

Optional equipment: Complete shore service connections $235, 4.0-kw generator $1,995, audible alarm gas sniffer $290, Monomatic toilet w/dockside discharge $395, complete flying bridge $1,875, air conditioning $1,295 to $2,800, 25-pound anchor w/1008 line $60, Bimini top $250, fender $13, 8' aluminum boat hook $10, compass 4" w/chrome binnacle $72, radio antenna bracket $45, dockside fresh-water connection $80, launch and make-ready $500, etc.

Pacemaker Drift-R-Cruz

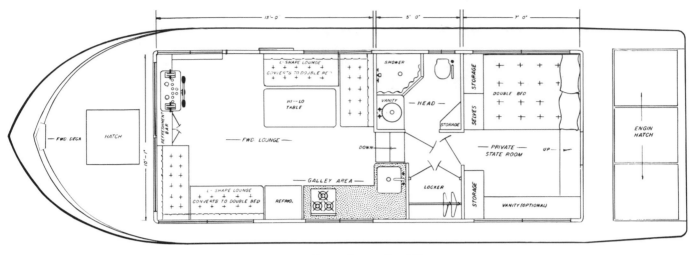

Diagram of River Queen Star*Stream

■ **River Queen**, P.O. Box 379, Douglas, Michigan 49406.

Model and specifications: Star*Stream 40, steel hull and cabin construction, length 40′, beam 13′, draft 19″, freeboard forward and aft 50″ and 30″, catwalks 14″, fore deck 8′ x 13′, stern deck 4′ x 13′, cabin 26′ x 10′, fuel capacity 42 gal, water capacity 42 gal, sleeps 8. Power options and prices: Single 225-hp Chrysler I/O $19,992, Twin 115-hp Chrysler I/O $23,900, Volvo 270-hp I/O $25,600, and Twin 225-hp Chrysler V-drive $26,500.

Standard equipment: Collision bulkhead forward, 5 bulkheads aft, 8 mooring cleats, bow spray rail and seat, complete lighting system, ship's bell and electric horn, mooring lines, anchor and line, choice of 4 carpet colors, complete head, adequate storage space.

Model: Newport 50, steel hull, cabin, and deck, length 50′, beam 15′, draft 3′8″, freeboard forward and aft 60″ and 36″, catwalks 18″, forward deck 8′5″ x 15′, stern deck 15′ x 8′ 5″, cabin 32′ x 12′, fuel capacity 100 gal (per engine), water capacity 100 gal.

Standard equipment: In addition to most of above, the following: Power steering, folding mast w/light, rudder position indicator, zinc hull anodes, deluxe pilot seat, refreshment bar in forward cabin, AC-DC interior lighting, 14-cu-ft electric refrigerator.

Optional equipment: Fuel level indicator $56, muffler $140, long-range fuel tank 100 gal $224, power steering $296, spare prop $68, air conditioner $660 and $740, depth indicator $240, heater $120, hailer w/fog signal $220, zinc hull anodes $20, upper command station $1,245, etc.

■ **SeaLine Boats Inc.**, 4320 Jackson Hwy., Sheffield, Alabama 35660

Model and specifications: SeaLine 50, fiberglass construction, length 50′, beam 14′, cabin 32′ x 10′4″, fore deck 10′, aft deck 8′, fuel capacity 160 gal, water capacity 110 gal, headroom 6′3″, folding catwalks (for road shipment). Power: Single 225-hp Chrysler Marine engine w/out drive. Price: $39,839.

Standard equipment: Color coded 12-V wiring system, 60 amp. breaker box, complete lighting system, galley, and head, hide-a-bed in wheelhouse, 20-pound propane tank, pad and carpet, safety glass, Roman shades, etc.

Optional equipment: Prices N/A for the following: Fold-up catwalks, generator, electric range, hanging lockers, 50' shore power cord, air conditioner, end tables w/drawers, ice maker, bar light, fixture and mirror, depth finder, and flying bridge.

■ **Sea Rover Marine,** 1301 Bay St. S.E., St. Petersburg, Florida 33701.

Model and specifications: Sea Rover 36, fiberglass construction, length 37'9", beam 12', draft 19", freeboard forward and aft 54" and 44", cabin 24' x 9', headroom 6'6", fuel capacity 65 gal, water capacity 50 gal, sleeps 6 to 10. Power: 225-hp Chrysler engine. Price: $20,000.

Standard equipment: Complete galley, head, and lighting equipment, large chart table, deluxe carpeting and paneling, circuit breakers for 115-V system, bilge blower, molded fiberglass deck box and seat, teak handrails, sliding windows w/tempered safety glass, color-coded wiring harness, shore power cable and adapter, shag carpeting color-coordinated w/drapes and furniture, water tested w/commissioning record.

Diagram of SeaLine

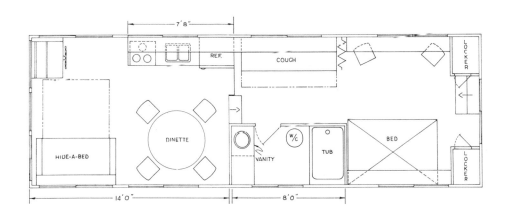

Diagram of Sea Rover

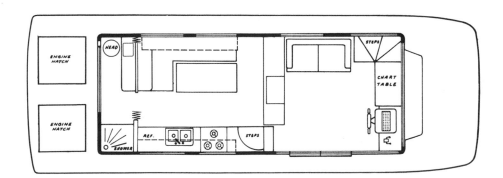

Optional equipment: N/A.

Note: The Sea Rover is available in 3 different floor plans w/a variety of interior, exterior combinations, sleeping accommodations, and furniture arrangement. The models include the Super Sea Rover, Executive, and Heritage.

■ **Sport-Craft,** P.O. Box 351, Perry, Florida 32347.

Model and specifications: Sport-Craft 300, fiberglass construction, length 30', beam 12', cabin 18' x 9', headroom 6'8" sundeck 10', walkway 1'6", wt 9,500 pounds, sleeps 8 or more. Power options: MerCruiser I/O: 270-325-T/165, or OMC I/O: T/155-T/165. Price: $14,926.

Standard equipment: Pilothouse raised w/full forward and aft vision, rails on sundeck, sides, bow and stern, complete galley and head, drapes, carpeting, paneling, complete lighting system w/110-V dockside connections, 80-gal fuel tank, water capacity 39 gal, electric gas gauge, etc.

Model: Sport-Craft 240, fiberglass, length 24'6", beam 8', cabin 15' x 7'2", sundeck 24', forward deck 5'2", aft deck 4'4", wt 2,500 pounds, sleeps 5. Power: Outboard only. Price: $4,995.

Standard equipment: Bow, stern, and sundeck railings, running lights, sliding glass windows w/screens and curtains, hanging closets, complete head, galley, and lighting systems, propane tank, etc.

Optional equipment: Prices N/A. Electric head and chlorinator, power steering, Kohler electric power plant, hot water heater, air conditioner, helmsman seat, foam flotation, etc.

■ **Stardust Cruiser Mfg. Co.,** P.O. Box 5262, Chattanooga, Tennessee 37406.

Model and specifications: Stardust 40, steel hull, length 40', beam 11', depth of hull 31", cabin 8' x 8', forward deck 10' x 11', water capacity 40 gal, wt 8,000 pounds. Power options: 120- to 225-hp MerCruiser, $3,295 to $4,995, and 120- to 245-hp OMC, $3,295 to $4,695. All engine installations include: gas tank w/gauges, prop, bilge pump and blower, battery, cables, control heads, and instrument panel.

Standard equipment: Tile floors, aluminum sides, sundeck, swim ladder, complete head and galley, 3 separate lighting systems, 40-gal water tank.

Model: Stardust 44, steel hull, length 44', beam 12', hull depth 3', forward deck 12' x 12', living room 10' x 16', water capacity 100 gal, wt 12,000 pounds. Power options: Same as above. Price: $17,500.

Standard equipment: Same as the Stardust 40 model, but note the increased dimensions of living space.

Model: Stardust 52, steel hull, length 52', beam 13', depth of hull 3', forward deck 12' x 13', living room 10' x 20', wt 16,000 pounds, water tank 100 gal. Power Twin 270 hp. Price: $21,500. (A similar 52' deep-V fiberglass model is offered at $22,500.)

Standard equipment: Same as the above models, plus the following: deluxe medicine cabinet, built-in marble top sink w/molded fiberglass tub and shower and electric hot water heater, queen-size hide-a-bed, Micarta top table w/4 chairs.

ABOVE: *Stardust*
BELOW: *Sport-Craft 300*

Model: Stardust 57, steel hull, length 57', beam 13', depth of hull 3', forward deck 12' x 13', living room 10' x 20', 100-gal water tank, wt 20,000 pounds. Power options: Same as above. Price: $26,500.

Standard equipment: All the features in the above models, along with customized floor plans.

Optional equipment for all Stardust models: Power options from $3,295 to $4,695, power plants 2,500 kw at $1,475 to 7,500 kw at $2,595, air conditioner and heater $750, spotlight 5" $265, butane stove w/oven $245, baseboard electric heat $425, compass $50, flybridge $5,000, etc.

■ Uniflite Inc., P.O. Box 1095, Bellingham, Washington 98225.

Model and specifications: Yacht-Home 36, fiberglass construction

ABOVE: *Uniflite Yacht-Home*
LEFT: *Watercraft*

w/Underwriters Laboratory seal for fire-retardant hull, length 36′3″, beam 12′4″, cabin 16′ x 10′, freeboard forward and aft 41″ and 36″, aft deck 5′6″ x 12′4″, headroom 6′8″, fuel capacity 108 gal, water capacity 50 gal, height above waterline 9′5″, sleeps 6, wt 11,500 pounds. Power: 225-hp V-D; TS 1½, and optional 1-gear Diesel, and 225-hp I/O engine. Price: $28,300 and $30,800.

Standard equipment: Convertible dinette and settee, complete galley and head, and lighting system, wrap-around safety glass windshield, wood paneling, carpeting, upholstery and draperies, 15″ wide double railed walk-arounds, self-bailing aft cockpit, canopied forward deck, modified V-hull bottom and hard chine for lateral stability and responsiveness to helm, Morse steering and controls, windshield wiper, sliding glass doors and windows, bilge pump and blower, bronze shaft and rudder, fuzed electric system, ship's bell and horn, etc.

Optional equipment (prices on request): Alarm systems, battery switchover and charger, cigar lighter, chart light, Bimini top cover, Ritchie compass dp60, dockside power cord, fishing rod holder, fathometer Raytheon DE736, generators, heaters, spare prop, stereo system, C.B. radio Johnson 100, electric winch, bonded zinc plate, various instruments, etc.

■ **Watercraft Inc.,** Pumping Station Rd., Gallatin, Tennessee 37066.

Model and specifications: Watercraft 45, aluminum hull, cabin, windows, and railings, length 45', beam 12', freeboard forward and aft 36" and 34", draft 12", aft deck 7'6" long, forward deck 8' long, cabin 9'6" x 30', headroom 6'8", catwalk width 15", sleeps 8 in 3 separate sleeping compartments. Power: Twin 225-hp Chrysler V-Drive, or Twin 165-hp MerCruisers. Price: $27,995.

Standard equipment: 120-gal pressure system, complete lighting w/ 12-V and 110-V systems, anchor cleats and line, 3 fire extinguishers, complete galley and head, shag carpeting throughout, collision bulkhead forward, choice of 4 interior and exterior color schemes, stereo system w/4 speakers, etc.

Model: Watercraft 50, aluminum construction, length 50'6", beam 14', freeboard forward and aft 36" and 34", draft 12," aft deck 7'6", forward deck 8', cabin 11' x 35', headroom 6'8", catwalk width 18", sleeps 8. Power: Twin 225 V-D Chrysler engine. Price: $29,995.

Standard equipment: Same as the above model.

Model: Watercraft 55, aluminum, length 55', beam 14', freeboard forward and aft 36" and 34", draft 12", aft deck 7'6" long, forward deck 8' long, cabin 40' x 11', headroom 6'8", catwalk width 18", sleeps 8. Power: Twin 225-hp V-D Chryster or Twin 165-hp MerCruisers. Price: quoted upon request.

Standard equipment: Same as 45' model.

Model: Watercraft 60, aluminum, length 60', beam 14", freeboard forward and aft 36" and 34", draft 12", aft deck 7'6" long, forward deck 8' long, cabin 45' x 11", headroom 6'8", catwalk width 18", sleeps 8. Power: Twin 225-hp V-D Chrysler. Price: quoted upon request.

Standard equipment: Same as 45' model.

Optional equipment (for all Watercraft models): Automatic bilge pump $60, Command bridge w/power steering, air conditioner $695, electric stove $185, generator 7.5 kw Kohler $2,600, central vacuum system $275, depth sounder $195, engine hour meter $26, extra fire extinguisher $20, bridge to bridge intercom $75, spare prop $129, windshield wiper $45, extra water tank 100 gal $250, factory launch and make-ready $300.

■ **Whitcraft Houseboat Division AMF,** 24 Laird St., Winona, Minnesota 55987.

Whitcraft 50

Model and specifications: Whitcraft 50, plan A, fiberglass construction w/modified deep-V hull, length 50', beam 12'8", draft 3'1", freeboard forward and aft 4'8" and 4', sleeps 10 to 12, headroom 6'5", aft cabin 20'4" x 11'4", forward cabin 8'10" x 8'9", salon 13'8" x 8'10", forward 6'4" x 11'6", sundeck 16'8" x 11', aft deck 7'11" x 11'7", estimated wt 24,200 pounds, fuel capacity 240 gal (gas) and 344 gal (Diesel fuel), water capacity 100 gal. Power: Twin 280-hp V-8 Chrysler. Optional: Twin 330-hp V-8 Chrysler, Twin 300-hp Chris-Craft V-8s, and 160-hp Perkins Diesel. Price: $67,000.

Note: An optional floor plan B, for extra room, is available, and includes a double cabin, sleeps 8 in 2 private staterooms.

Standard equipment: Anchor light, queen-size bed, bilge pump and blower, foam cushions, wall-to-wall carpeting, draperies, complete galley w/high-pressure laminates on all counter tops and dinette table, 2 heads w/showers, fuel and water gauges, complete lighting system w/dockside hookups, lounge and lunch bar, mast w/anchor light, tinted safety glass, screened windows and sliding doors, 4 wardrobe closets, teak paneling, nonslip, nonskid decks, etc.

Model: Whitcraft 45, fiberglass, length 45', beam 12', draft 3'2", freeboard forward and aft 4'8" and 4', sleeps 8, headroom 6'6", cabin 28' x 9', forward deck 9'2" x 12', aft deck 7'8 x 12', side decks 28'2 x 1'4", estimated wt 21,100 pounds, fuel capacity 240 gal (gas) and 216 gal (Diesel fuel), water capacity 100 gal. Power: Twin 225-hp V-Drive Chrysler. Optional: Twin 280-hp V-Drive Chrysler and 160-hp Perkins Diesel. Price: N/A.

Optional equipment: Air conditioner $1,220 and $2,085, battery combinations $94 to $134, bilge pump $105, compass 3½" $70, cradle $396, depth sounder $220, engine alarm system $375, flying bridge w/dual controls, gas fume detector $171, generators $2,750 to $3,999, electric heater $100, mufflers $300 to $510, spare prop $149, pilot chair $176, searchlight w/2 jacks $80, stereo system w/4 speakers, swim platform w/ladder $800, shorewater connection $88, etc.

11

Floating Homes and Trailerable Houseboats

There are approximately 9 million recreational boats in our country, of which 20 percent are estimated to be of size and shape that permits living aboard; thousands of Americans are doing just that, living aboard their craft for weekends and vacation periods, but a growing number are living permanently on the water. Where there is a promise of sheltered water for the houseboat, and a "star to steer her by," people have dropped anchor and have established a residence on water.

The floating home requires a substantial hull; it is anchored or permanently fixed near shore and sometimes cemented into place. The boat is, in essence, a home built on water instead of on a plot of ground. In some regions, the owners of floating homes are called "liver-inners" and they seem to have solved their personal housing shortage.

The "Why?" of a Floating Home. A sailor's love of the water, the mystique of the sea, pursuing distant horizons, do not accurately indicate the motivations for buying and living aboard a floating home. The reason is primarily economic, followed closely by an insufficiency of housing. Reasons for the soaring cost of building sites and the shortage of reasonably priced conventional housing in desired locations become obvious when we realize that double the number of houses and apartments we are currently building is the projected need for the remainder of this decade. Many houseboats can be bought much below the price of the cheapest home, and their appointments are as modern as those of the up-to-date aprtment.

Opposition. Some municipal authorities, in boating areas, object to the proliferation of floating homes. They claim that the concentration of boats with lack of standards in upkeep, housekeeping, and garbage and sewage disposal creates waterfront ghettos. Some floating homes are actually built from the flotsam and jetsam found floating on the water or along the bank: Plywood, timbers, styrofoam, fish nets, floats, and the like are used for the shantyboat-type of residence.

The U.S. Coast Guard has no jurisdiction over watercraft that is docked, beached, stored, trailered, etc., even if it is violating zoning laws, is untitled, unsafe, untaxed, and unlicensed.

Permanent floating home colonies are found in many sections of the country, but nowhere are they as popular and numerous as in California.

■ **The Sacramento River delta,** an inland maze of waterways, serves the liver-inners in a motley array of craft, from boxy plywood structures mounted on oil drums and powered by outboard motors to high-powered yachts with swimming pools and recreation rooms with bars. Some owners with imagination and artistic bent create floating homes of striking beauty. They have few traditional guidelines to follow, and as a result, give free, sometimes wild, rein to their talents.

■ **Sausalito,** on the littoral of San Francisco Bay, has a floating home colony of free souls, who have broken away from 8-to-5 jobs, possessions, freeways, and responsibility in general to evolve a way that many call "way out." Their homes are old scows and crate-like boats, anchored or aground; and access is by swaying and rickety planks. Some boats are decorated with bright paint, colored glass, dried or plastic flora, fish nets, and the symbolic objects of the owners' creation. They live with little concern for the outside world, but they must enter it on occasion to sell their trinkets and found-art. The permanent residents are a closely knit group, born of a common life-style and outlook and the need to put up a solid front in the face of opposition.

City elders, particularly real estate developers, realize that the waterfront, the far-side prominent peninsula, and warm mists drifting from the Pacific offer a South Sea type of beauty and languor, ideal for shoreline and hillside residence—the type that Californians compete and pay heavily for.

■ **Long Beach** Marina looks like a college campus or prideful city park, so well landscaped and maintained is the facility. So popular is this live-in marina that there is a wait of 8 to 10 years to get called. The 1,800 small boat slips, neatly clean and brightly painted, berth many floating homes that will never navigate the ocean blue. An old salt would miss the sight of seagoing preparations—tinkering with the engine, drying nets, coiling lines, and polishing brass. Instead, owners boast of their freedom from land living with its lawn and landscaping chores, of the satisfying identification with the sea, and of the very low rental. The explanation: Long Beach receives royalties from offshore oil, and one of the stipulations is that the city's share of royalties must be ploughed back into the improvement of the waterfront.

■ **Portofino** is 15 miles north of Long Beach in mileage, but a thousand miles away in nautical philosophy. The 200-slip marina draws a younger and more adventurous group that knows the open sea. There are everywhere the smells of tar, rope, oil, and the general disorder of a working dock. Crews of husband, wife, and children can be seen swabbing, scraping, and painting in preparation to going to sea.

The children become involved in the operation and maintenance aspects of their floating home, and for them fishing, swimming, snorkeling may replace Little League or ballet. As for family pets, cats, dogs, and rabbits are often replaced by pipefish, crabs, snails, and other ocean creatures. All crew members look forward to the extended trip during summer vacation, cruising down the coast to Baja Mexico.

THE LUXURIOUS AND ELEGANT FLOATING HOME

Imagine all the appointments, furniture, appliances, and other niceties that symbolize for many the good life, the "right side of the tracks," and you gain an insight into what a posh floating home is really like.

Marine engineering and sophisticated home construction are responsible for a new way of life: living aboard a status-symbol craft that is equally fulfilling and rewarding to professionals, swinging bachelors, and businessmen. They enjoy the refinements of the urban milieu, residing near their work and sources of entertainment, yet with a semblance of privacy—much better than the suburban boondocks.

Aboard the posh floating home, the range of dress is from the bikini to evening gown and from swim trunks to tails; the form of entertainment is from cocktail parties at sunset to a group discussion of local

Floating home owners with imagination and artistic bent give free rein to their talents, as this entrance from the shore side indicates.

and world politics, from barbecued steaks on the aft deck to a gourmet dinner indoors; and throughout the demeanor can range from the hippish to the staid.

Looking into some of the distinctions that characterize this glamorous member of the houseboat family, we find that it does not move on its own power, there's no engine, compass, anchor, or navigation instruments. However, beyond that, its features place it in a boating fleet all its own and unique in the history of seafaring.

In the context of a typical houseboat, the expensive and artistic floating home doesn't at all look like a houseboat. Its superstructure consists of land-based architectural styles as featured in suburban subdivisions: colonial, Tudor, modern, Spanish, French, and combinations that defy identification. The roofs are mansard, flat adobe style, and gabled. The exteriors are shingled and paneled with wood, aluminum, and composition board, which are placed horizontally, vertically, or diagonally. Exterior features include overhang roofs, hanging and deck flower boxes, trellises, and various levels with outside patio, solarium, and swimming pool. But it is the interior of a floating home that really brings out its elegant appointments.

The designer and builder of expensive floating homes offers commensurate adequate and elegant living space: two or three levels (in the 50 x 30-foot class, more or less), living room, two or three bedrooms, galley, den, two tub and shower bathrooms, inside/outside patio, and a topside solarium.

The interior can include open-beam ceiling; spiral staircase; floor coverings of tile, wood, parquet, or oriental rugs; and matching drapes and wallpaper with nautical patterns.

The kitchen serves the gourmet cook with a three-burner stove or radar range, an eye-level oven, refrigerator, ice maker, dishwasher, indoor hibachi, and outdoor barbecue.

Other features include powder room with full-length mirror, marble table tops, antiqued mirror, brass candelabrum, nautical antiques, leather chairs, washer-dryer, vacuum cleaner, and floor polisher.

For communication and entertainment, the houseboat is equipped with telephone, intercom, radio, TV, hi-fi, and tape recorder.

Probably, one of the few designer-builders in the United States that can accommodate the customer with a floating home replete with the above, and more, is Ray Lore, of Sea View Floating Homes, Miami, Florida. His theory of nautical design indicates that the floating home must ride high and dry; it must be wide and stable, with tons of ballast; it must include liberal dimensions for the galley and main cabin; and the hull must be leakproof. No models are built on speculation; all are custom made, and the prospective customer engages in extensive preplanning conferences with all craftsmen involved, hashing out tastes versus price, appointments versus practicality, and design features versus dimension limitations. Only when all questions and differences are resolved does construction begin, with about 90 days for delivery. The functional homes serve as floating clinics or motels, and offer office headquarters for doctors, architects, and lawyers. Price: $30,000 to $200,000.

Floating Home Problems. All is not champagne and lobster with the

Aboard the posh floating home, the range of dress is from the bikini to an evening gown, with food from a steak barbecue on the aft deck to a gourmet dinner in the galley.

The Sea View custom models of floating homes have become status symbols, offering year-round living in southern waters.

floating home arrangement. There are problems in finding suitable marinas, waste disposal, and opposition from city officials. Upkeep costs are as much, and more, than for the land-based home. A leak in the hull cannot be ignored or easily patched. The haul-out is the only way to repair the hull or other damage. The maintenance chores of scraping and painting are a bit more difficult; after all, you can't prop a stepladder to paint an outside wall. The phone, water supply, electricity, and refuse pick-up may not be dependable. The children have fewer playmates. Strong winds can clear your deck of all furniture and other loose items. But floating home owners insist that the advantages and pleasures exceed by far the disadvantages.

THE TRAILERABLE HOUSEBOAT

The trailerable houseboat has many advantages; it can be used as a conventional camper-trailer on land and a houseboat on water, giving, in effect, two recreational vehicles for the price of one. Kept within the required 8-foot width, the trailerable can be towed along the nation's highways and launched anywhere on water that looks suitable. The trailerable can be berthed at home to save storage expenses, and it is always available for those endless cleaning tasks and maintenance problems that crop up.

This versatile newcomer to the outdoor recreation scene of off-road vehicles and craft becomes amphibious at the water's edge. After arrival, there's no transfer of food, clothing, or gear; it's all aboard. The trailer backs up to the launching ramp, and the chauffeur of the car-trailer rig becomes the skipper of a seagoing houseboat. Should the weather get frisky, it's but a matter of hauling out the boat to a nearby trailer park or campground and connecting up for water and electricity as any other trailer.

The only limits imposed on the trailerable houseboat are 8 feet maximum width, and 35 feet maximum length, which places it in the moderate (original) price range. Subsequent operational expenses are also less than for the conventional houseboat. As to trailering, there's little concern in hauling a 3-ton houseboat with the conventional car. A boat 32 feet long, weighing 3 tons, imposes only 300 pounds of tongue weight on the hitch. All in all, the trailerable houseboat offers an ideal craft for retired and childless couples. For sleeping needs beyond two, check the specifications of the firms listed below. The price range will be $4,000 to $12,000, but a high or low price is not valid per se; you must know what the price includes.

Buyer's Guide. The firms offering trailerable houseboats are here listed with a reference to their salient features. The limitation of size (8' wide, 35' long) in these camper-cruisers results in economical packages, but at the same time, inside furnishings, accommodations, and equipment in general, may be affected by the less liberal dimensions.

■ Cutter (Division of Cargile, Inc.), Box 11499, 999 Polk St., Nashville, Tennessee 37211.

Features: 28′ Cutter. One-piece molded fiberglass hull, and hardtop cabin w/sunroof opening, and safety handrails. Command bridge w/full windshield. Sleeps 2 in forward stateroom, 2 on command bridge, 2 in converted dinette. Pressure water system w/filter, shower, marine head. Large 6′ kitchen counter w/sink, 3-burner range and oven. Self-bailing aft cockpit, bilge blower. Complete lighting system inside and running. Approximate speed 35 mph. Many practical items offered as options. Prices: $12,995 to $14,395 w/single engine; $15,445 and $16,355 w/twin engines.

■ **Glendale Plastics**, Box 158, 145 Queen St., Strathroy, Ontario, Canada.
Features: Two models, Hobo Hardtop and Hobo Fisherman. All-fiberglass hull and interior. Low-profile styling. Combination of cruiser,

ABOVE: *Cutter*
RIGHT: *Hobo*

camper, and fast runabout which planes to adequate speed for water skiing. Sleeps 4. Galley, head, and running lights. Windows w/radiused corners and built-in screens. Outboard motor 85 hp. Recessed storage for gasoline tanks. Captain's wheel mounted on molded console. Shore power connection. Retractable interior steps. Options: Foredeck canopy, drapes, horn, windshield wiper, carpet runner. Price: N/A.

■ **Kennedy Houseboats, Inc.,** Box 338, Miller, South Dakota 57362.
  Features: Two models, 27' Mate and 30' Skipper. Marine alloy aluminum pontoons w/tubular frame construction. Exterior-grade plywood on decks and roof. Approved lighting. Interior walnut vinyl paneling. Recirculating marine toilet. Wardrobe closet, vanity and mirror. Drapes. 2-burner stove, sink, laminated cabinet top. Sleeps 4, on vinyl foam mattress, cloth covered and zippered. Access ladder to sundeck. Water tank 30 gal, electric horn. Options: Deck enclosure, heater, refrigerator, etc. Price: $4,995 for Mate, $5,695 for Skipper.

■ **Sea Camper,** Box 1196, Green Cove Springs, Florida 32043.
  Features: Tri-hull, cabin, and interior of hand-laid-up fiberglass. Three distinct areas, lounge, forward, and helm. Wall-to-wall indoor/outdoor

Kennedy

SeaCamper

carpeting. Tinted sliding windows w/curtains and screens. Sleeps 6 on upholstered mattress cushions. Speed up to 38 mph w/165-hp engine. Complete electric system, galley w/3-burner propane stove, icebox, stainless steel sink. Head w/exhaust fan and shower. Horn, bilge pump. Options: Flybridge, complete trim package, storage package, equipment package, trailer. Price: $9,796 w/140-hp engine.

■ **Steury Corp.,** 2827 Rupp Dr., Box 5197, Ft. Wayne, Indiana 46805.
Features: Four models 18' to 23' w/fiberglass hull, deep-V bottom. Sleeps 2 to 8 w/5" foam cushions. Color-coordinated drapes, shag carpeting, and upholstery. Complete head, galley, and lighting systems. Electric and water hook-ups. Elevated pilot cockpit. Options: Drapes, air conditioning, heater, etc. Price: $10,825 to $12,095 depending upon engine option and size of model.

■ **Trail or Float Corp.,** Box 545, Gresham, Oregon 97030.
Features: Trail or Float 25' model embodies a unique concept of a land trailer w/2 fiberglass pontoons that are carried topside of the trailer, and once the launching site is reached, a hydraulic pump is used to swing out and lower them to the bottom sides of the trailer

Steury

where they are locked into place. The operation increases the beam width from 7'6" on land, to a width of 13' when launched. Patented in the U.S. and Canada. Sleeps 4 to 6. Outboard motor 40 hp is recommended, and gives speed of 10 mph. Complete galley w/3-burner stove, icebox, sink, 20-gal tank. Navigation and inside lighting. Options: Electric hydraulic pump, remote-control searchlight, carpeting, heater, 3 toilet options, shower, holding tank, carpeting. Price: $5,250.

■ **Yachtster, Inc.,** Box 507, Salina, Kansas 67401.

Features: Three models, 28' Mark, 28' Mark II, 31' Mark III, Cathedral deep-V fiberglass hull. All-electric kitchen, 4-cu.-ft. icebox, 2-burner stove, stainless steel sink, water tank, and pump. Interior w/avocado hickory paneling, crimson red wall-to-wall carpeting, zebra-cushioned upholstery. Dual-voltage lighting, shore hook-ups. Speed of 40 mph w/optional power, diesel or V-8 jet drive. Low profile. Patent applied for Automatic Flying Bridge that is electrically raised and lowered. Sleeps 8 to 10 w/foam cushion mattress. Head, horn, mooring cleats. Price: $6,995 to $12,750, which includes all options and equipment in a complete package. Note: For the do-it-yourselfer, bare fiberglass hulls 28' are available for back-yard builders who wish to complete and customize their own cabin, etc. Price: $3,500.

■ **Yukon-Delta, Inc.,** 405 Jay Dee St., Elkhart, Indiana 46514.

Features: 25' model w/fiberglass tri-hull. All inside and outside walls w/styrofoam insulation, laminated and pressed. Load capacity 4,000 pounds. Road height of 8'7" offers little wind drag. Complete lighting system. Galley w/2-burner stove, ice chest, 12-gal water system w/holding tank. Deck ladder, front and top railing. All wiring w/ground. Sleeps 4. Outboard motor 50 hp is recommended. Options: N/A. Price: $3,995 less trailer.

RIGHT: *Yachtster*
BELOW: *Yukon-Delta*

PONTOON BOATS

There is a fine line between the standard pontoon boat and the pontoon houseboat. The pontoon boat is an open platform craft with the dual cylindrical aluminum or steel pontoons supporting a sturdy deck, circled by a railing and a canopy overhead. It can be towed to a desirable location, but usually it is powered by an outboard motor. The simple craft serves as an ideal family or group boat, fishing barge, diving platform, water taxi, sightseeing craft, and so on. The open boat is inexpensive and offers for many a springboard to houseboating. The simple but functional craft, with some labor and the purchase of options, grows and grows. A stove is added, then sink and water connections, icebox, wet bar, helmstand with mechanical steering controls, compass, horn, spotlight, swivel chairs, etc. In the evolution, the canopy frame is enclosed with fabric, wood paneling, or sheet aluminum. A

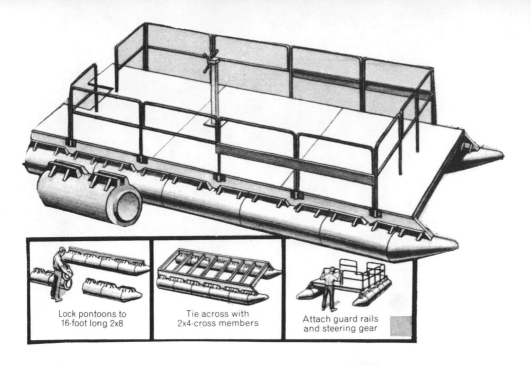

Lock pontoons to
16-foot long 2x8

Tie across with
2x4-cross members

Attach guard rails
and steering gear

ABOVE: *Diagram Sears, Roebuck & Co.*
RIGHT: *Kayot*
BELOW: *Sylvan*

self-contained john is concealed by a circular shower curtain. Now the craft is prepared for inclement weather, for overnight camping, and other activities—indeed it is a houseboat.

Buyer's Guide. The manufacturers of pontoon boats offer utility along with eye-appealing decks and tops. The models may be used as purchased, or converted as discussed above.

■ **Sears, Roebuck & Co.,** Dept. 703, 303 E. Ohio St., Chicago, Illinois 60611.

A 17′ pontoon boat kit which includes everything except the lumber. There are 12 interlocking polyethylene pontoons bolted to 2″ x 8″ beams to form a 8′ x 12′ deck. The boat accepts outboard motors up to 25 hp. The kit includes 12 pontoons that are watertight; will not crack, chip, rust; and are unaffected by solvents, acids, and fuels. Also included: motor mount assembly, 16 brackets for cross-beams, hardware, railing, steering gear, helmstation, and complete instructions for assembly. Send for free plans 39 AV 7565. Price: $489.

■ **Kayot, Inc.,** 450 Baker Bldg., Minneapolis, Minnesota 55402.

Eight models w/either steel or aluminum pontoons from 16′ to 28′ long, w/sandwich sidewall construction, and interlocking aluminum handrails. Features include wheel and binnacle, tiller cable steering, vinyl deck, gas tank, and battery holder. The top boats in the line include a galley, wet bar, icebox, 3-burner stove, 2 upholstered davenos. The optional canvas enclosure converts the boat into a tent trailerable for camping, hunting, and other trips. Options available. Price: $745 to $3,950.

■ **Sylvan Industries, Inc.,** Goshen, Indiana 46526.

Six models feature 22″-dia pontoons w/upswept nose cones to protect against beaching damage and deflect spray from deck. Also included: hard top, sundeck, diving platform, fuel tank, upholstered furniture, steering stand, swivel helmsman's chair, color-coordinated furniture, and power range from 5 to 100 hp. Price: N/A.

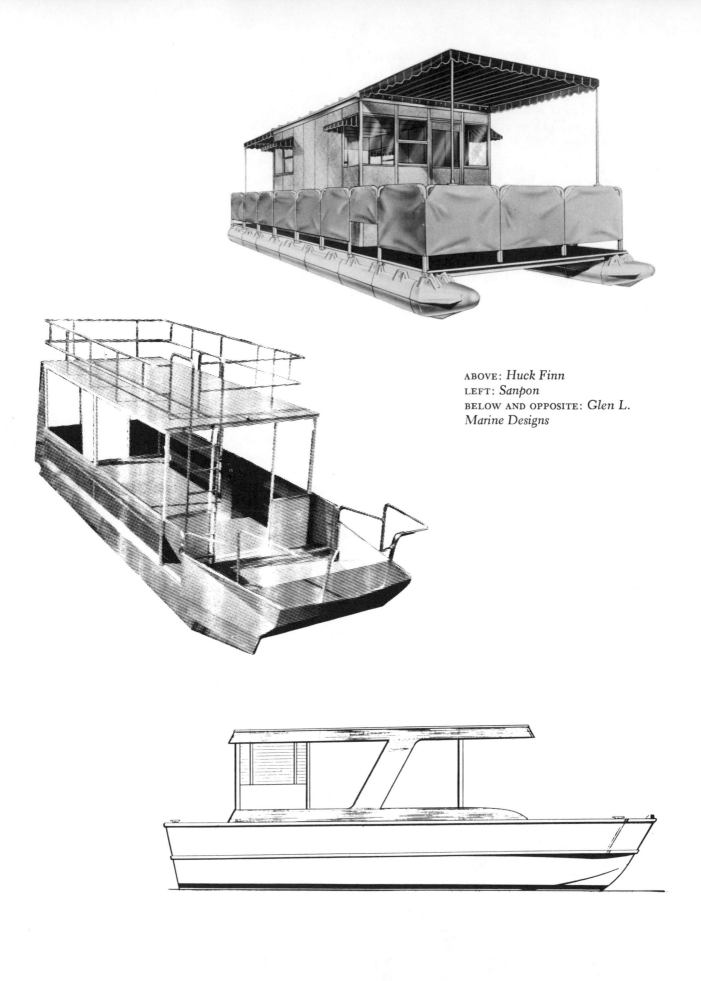

ABOVE: *Huck Finn*
LEFT: *Sanpon*
BELOW AND OPPOSITE: *Glen L.
Marine Designs*

■ **Kennedy Houseboats, Inc.,** Box 338, Miller, South Dakota 57362.

Four open-deck boats w/all-aluminum octagon-shaped pontoons, all-aluminum frame, anodized aluminum railings w/baked enamel panels, sundeck rails, 3 safety gates, carpeting, adjustable motor mount, and mechanical steering. Price: $1,155 to $1,525.

■ **Huck Finn, Inc.,** 8333 Sunset Rd. N.E., Minneapolis, Minnesota 55432.

Four different size kits 24′ to 42′ w/a power range of 25- to 55-hp outboard motor. Also included: motor mount assembly, pontoons w/spray-deflecting nose at each end. All components sold separately. Write for "Part Description" sheet.

■ **Sanpon Boats,** 2978 S. Cherry Ave., Fresno, California 93706.

Pontoon boat rigs w/a deck, ready to enclose and customize by the home craftsman. One model is constructed so that a Toyota or Datsun camper can be driven aboard to evolve into an instant houseboat. The deluxe model includes a dimension of 8′ x 30′ w/marine alloy pontoons, decking, motor mount, deck trim, vinyl carpet. Price: $1,150 to $2,950.

■ **Glen L. Marine Designs,** 9152-HG, Rosecrans, Bellflower, California 90706.

Houseboat plans only for the amateur builder. Complete plans and patterns are available for 25′ and 33′ Delta Queen, and 20′ Gypsy models of cruising houseboats. The plans give step-by-step instructions. The patterns are full size and facilitate the plywood construction. Price: $28 for Gypsy set; $49 for Delta Queen set of plans and patterns.

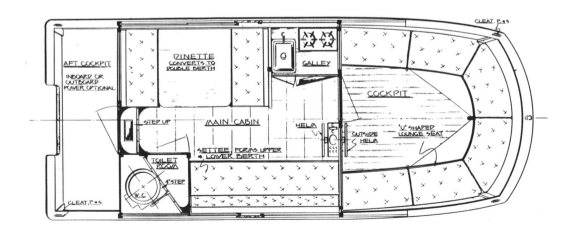

12

Houseboat Rentals
in the Northeast
and Southeast

A boating trend that fills the bill for a family vacation, or any group for that matter, is the houseboat rental. It offers an economical recreation package that abounds in possibilities for the enjoyment of many water-oriented experiences. And price-wise, a rental is no more expensive than an outing at the seashore, mountain, or forest resort.

Renting provides a good opportunity to learn the lore of houseboating, to test out a model, and to see if it will meet your needs. You'll learn preferences from the experience, how large a boat you will need, what type and how much power you should have, along with the model's general advantages or limitations.

Particularly if you are considering a model for purchase, you might ask the manufacturer to recommend a rental agency that uses their model. A two- or three-day shakedown rental cruise can be more meaningful and valuable than a demonstration run, dockside inspection, or sales pitch.

Rental rates are dependent upon the size of the boat, power plant, general condition, services, and location. Rental fees command a range from $185 to $800 (in the Caribbean) per week and cover everything except food and fuel and, in some cases, bedding. The cost, seemingly high, is for a facility that accommodates six to eight persons, and whether one or two families use the boat, the cost compares favorably with other types of vacation housing. The demand for houseboat rentals often exceeds the supply, so make your reservations well in advance. Discount rates are available in spring until June, and after Labor Day; some marinas offer 10 percent, others 20.

In the European housekeeping (economy) plan you rent the houseboat, do all your own cooking, and supply the food. The plan is popular with large families, and less expensive than a resort—and you can't dive into the water, or fish, from a resort roof. Mothers who are accustomed to vacationing in primitive cabins, where all the "back home" chores are evident but facilities inadequate, are impressed by the advantages of a houseboat: roomy interiors, carpeted floors, picture windows, drapes, three-burner range with oven, running water, built-in cabinets with tableware and cooking utensils. And should the weather get bad, there's plenty of floor area for the youngsters to sprawl on with their games, coloring books, and reading material.

For a higher rental rate you can go on the "outfitting plan"—ideal for the avid fishing family. In the plan one man acts as guide and crew and does all chores except cooking and housekeeping. Food is supplied, but you prepare it.

A deluxe executive plan, offered by a few rental agencies, provides the services of two persons—a full-time cook and guide. Food is provided, prepared, and served. There are no dishes to wash or beds to make—just communing with the sun and listening to the wind and waves as all go about their own personal projects.

Regardless of your boating experience, get all possible instruction from your rental agent before casting off on your own. Don't hurry the procedure. Ask many questions, even though they may seem inconsequential. With the guide at your side, practice docking, beaching, steering in tight places, and backing up. Even though this service is free, the agent doesn't mind; after all, he's concerned with your welfare and enjoyment, as well as the safety of his craft.

Though the shakedown will be in daylight, be sure to learn about the lighting: switches, running lights, and all. As wiring, controls, and the like differ among boats, learn about the one you're renting. Also, ask about water and gas gauges, stove and heaters, marine toilet, anchor, lines, and engine precautions.

The supplied charts of the watercourse, very much like road maps, are easy to understand. After the buoys and markers are explained— along with tips on where to go, what to see, and suggestions for night anchorage—the operator-guide climbs into his trailing boat and returns to the marina. You're on your own, but there's no concern, as you are well provisioned, fueled, and powered, and handling the boat offers little difficulty. Neither is there concern for emergencies—sickness, going aground, or getting lost—as most marina operators check the welfare of their customers by airplane or speedboat. And to ease your mind, the houseboat is covered by liability insurance.

Young men and women enjoy water activities: skiing, swimming, snorkeling by day, at night returning to marina dockage to go ashore, dine at some favorite café, then make the rounds where the action is.

For your floating vacation, houseboat rentals are here delineated by regions and states to give the renter references close to home and at a distance too.

NORTHEAST REGION

CONNECTICUT
East Coast Yacht Inc., S. Montowese St., Branford, 06405.

DELAWARE
Green Point Rent-A-Cruise, Box 4008, Wilmington, 19807. (302) 658-4318

DISTRICT OF COLUMBIA
Houseboat Rentals of Washington, D.C., Box 3678, Washington, 20007. (703) 524-4916.

MAINE
Houseboat Holidays, 262 Main St., Brunswick, 04011. (207) 729-3489.
Holidays Afloat, 83 Bay View St., Camden, 04843.

MARYLAND
Houseboats International Ltd., Fair Acres, Rt. 2, Annapolis, 20007. (301) 757-2000.
Houseboat Rentals of Baltimore, Box 3678, Washington, D.C. 20007. (703) 524-4916.
Wellwood Yacht Marina, N.E. River, Charlestown, 21914. (301) 287-8125.
Leisure Concepts Houseboat Rentals, Box 244, Ft. Washington, Pennsylvania 19034.
U-Skipper of Maryland, Rts. 50 & 301, Chester, 21619. (301) 643-5777.
Chesapeake Houseboats, Hances Point Cove, Box 78, North East, 21901. (301) 287-5614.
Anchor Away, Inc., 1264 Cresthaven Dr., Silver Spring, 20903. (301) 434-1019.
Rent-A-Cruise of Delimarva, Box 1466, Salisbury, 21801.

MASSACHUSETTS
Rent-A-Cruise of Buzzards Bay, Rts. 6 & 28, Buzzard's Bay, 02532. (617) 759-3388.
Houseboat Vacations, Inc., Longview Ave., Hinsdale, 01235. (413) 655-8140.

NEW HAMPSHIRE
Houseboat Vacations, Inc., 259 Gilsun St., Keene, 03431. (603) 352-8588.

NEW JERSEY
Captain Richie's Marina, Lacey Road, Forked River, 08731.
River Queen of the East, 1235 Fischer Blvd., Silverton, 08753. (201) 244-4004.
Osborne, Nassau, Citgo Marina, Rt. 166 & Crabb Rd., Toms River, 08753. (201) 244-1300.

NEW YORK
Bonnie Castle Yacht Basin, Box 368, Alexandria Bay, 13607. (315) 482-2526.
Charley's Rent-A-Cruise, Sisson St., Alexandria Bay, 13607.
Van's Motor Marine, Alexandria Bay, 13607. (315) 482-2271.

Suffolk Yacht Sales, 417 Fire Island Ave., Babylon, Long Island, 11702.

Rent-A-Cruise of Syracuse, Baldwinsville Boat Yard, 8½ Syracuse St., Baldwinsville, 13027.

Rent-A-Cruise of Brewerton, Ace Boat Yard, Young Rd., Brewerton, 10329.

Rent-A-Cruise of Catskill, Box 144, Catskill, 12414.

Russell's Boats, Ft. Montgomery, 10922. (914) 446-3440.

Sea Cove Houseboat Corp., 28 Shore Rd., Glen Cove, Long Island, 11542.

Bahia Mar Yacht Rentals, 183 Manson Ave., Great Kills, Staten Island, 10308.

Rent-A-Cruise of Finger Lakes, 620 Broad St., Horseheads, 14845.

Rent-A-Cruise of Hampton Bays, Box 18, Lake Grove, Long Island, 11755.

Rent-A-Cruise of Sacandage Lake, Old Route 30, Mayfield, 12117.

Carib Explorers, 375 Park Ave., New York, 10022. (212) 758-8365. (Virgin Islands rentals.)

Chris-Craft Aqua Home Rentals, 600 Madison Ave., New York, 10022. (212) 421-0207. (World-wide rentals.)

Hudson River Houseboat Rentals, 645 11th Ave., New York, 10019. (212) 787-0637.

Rent-A-Cruise of New York, 645 11th Ave., New York, 10036.

Dock and Coal Marina, Box 279, Plattsburgh, 12901. (518) 561-2800.

Moskowitz Marina, 20 Black Creek Rd., Rochester, 14623. (716) 464-8210.

Syosset United Rent-Alls, 110 Jackson Ave., Syosset, Long Island, 11791. (516) 921-2300.

Oswego Marina, 3522 James St., Syracuse, 13206. (315) 437-6651.

Van's Motor Marine, Houseboat Haven, Thousand Islands, 13607.

Hutchinson's Boat Works, Holland St. Boat Basin, Thousand Islands, 13607.

Smith Boys, 50 Fillmore Ave., Tonawanda, 14150.

SOUTHEAST REGION

ALABAMA

Dick Miree Marine, Box 445, Alabaster, 35507. (205) 663-3841.

Rent-A-Cruise, 4500 Fifth Ave., Birmingham, 35222. (205) 764-3500.

Rent-A-Cruise, Box 781, Florence, 35630. (205) 764-3500.

Cruises, Inc., 2105 Robinhood Dr., S.E., Huntsville, 35801.

U-Skipper Houseboat Rentals, Riverside Marina, Riverside, 25135. (205) 338-2291.

Tennessee River Rent-A-Cruise, Box 17, Sheffield, 35660. (205) 381-0971.

FLORIDA

Carefree Houseboat Rentals, Box 16, Bokeelia, 33922. (616) 926-7606.

Culver Boat Co., Box 147, Center Hill, 33514.

Outdoor Crafts, Box 899, Cocoa Beach, 32931.

Aloha Marina, 10 2nd St., Daytona Beach, 32017.

Rent-A-Houseboat, Box 6252, Daytona Beach, 32002. (904) 677-9231.

Flamingo Houseboats, Everglades National Park, Flamingo, 33030. (813) 695-3101.

Bahia Mar Yacht Rentals, Ft. Lauderdale, 33316.

Cargile Cruises, 1401 State Rd. 84, Ft. Lauderdale, 33316. (703) 524-4916.

Houseboat Holidays, Ft. Lauderdale, 33308.

Houseboat Rentals of Ft. Lauderdale, Box 3678, Washington, D.C. 20007. (703) 524-4916.

Rent-A-Cruise, Box 22506, Ft. Lauderdale, 33315. (305) 771-2142.

Rent-A-Cruise, 915 W. Sunrise Blvd., Ft. Lauderdale, 33311. (305) 764-2525.

Carefree Houseboat Rentals, 1011 San Carlos Blvd., Ft. Myers Beach, 33931. (813) 464-9413.

Sunshine State Houseboat Center, Box 4029, Ft. Myers Beach, 33931.

Cruis-A-Way Houseboat Rentals, 505 South St., Ft. Walton Beach, 32548.

Florida Houseboat Rentals, 523 Bahama Dr., Indian Harbour Beach, 32925. (305) 773-0141.

Surfside Six, Box 147, Kissimmee, 32741.

Florida Keys Houseboat Rentals, Box 1077, Marathon, 33050.

Holiday House Yachts, Box 771, Melbourne, 32935. (305) 773-1161.

Indian River Queen, 972 Terry Dr., Melbourne, 32935. (305) 254-3032.

Rent-A-Cruise of Miami, 2560 Bayshore Dr., Miami, 33133. (305) 448-5633.

Flotilla, Inc., Box 656, Naples, 33940. (813) 597-3911.

Grand Lagoon Marina, 5323 N. Lagoon Dr., Panama City, 32401.

Guy Rodgers Marine, Panama City, 32401.

Vacation Houseboat Rentals, 9184 54th Way N., Pinellas Park, 33565.

Rent-A-Cruise, Box 13015, Pt. Everglades, 33316.

Casey Key Houseboats, Box 15306, Sarasota, 33579.

Suncoast Houseboat Center, Box 5652, Sarasota, 33581. (813) 955-8272.

Aqua Home Rental, 3701 50th Ave., S., St. Petersburg, 33711.

Houseboat Harry, Box 308, Tavernier, 33070.

Rent-A-Cruise of the Keys, Box 38, Upper Key Largo, 33038.

Holiday Houseboats, West Palm Beach Marina, West Palm Beach, 33402.

GEORGIA

U-Skipper of Lake Lanier, Bald Ridge Marina, Box 805, Cumming, 30130. (404) 887-5309.

Lanier Flotels, Rt. 9, Box 427, Gainesville, 30501.

Harbor Light Marina, Lavonia, 30553. (404) 356-2975.

Houseboats of Marietta, Box 150, Marietta, 30060.

Brady Boat Works, Isle of Hope Marina, Box 6036, Savannah, 31405.

MISSISSIPPI

Rent-A-Cruise of Singing River, Box 565, Lucedale, 39452. (601) 947-3467.

Rent-A-Cruise, 900 Pine St., Suite 5, Vicksburg, 39180. (601) 636-8264.

NORTH CAROLINA

J. D. Cotter, Box 937, Washington, 27889.

Houseboat Rentals, Box 10718, Winston-Salem, 27108.

SOUTH CAROLINA

Rent-A-Cruise of Hartwell Lake, Rt. 3, Anderson, 29621.

Rent-A-Cruise of Charleston, Box 622, Charleston, 29042.

Rent-A-Cruise of Santee, Box 96, Santee, 29142.

TENNESSEE

Cypress Bay Resort, Rt. 2, Buchanan, 39222.

Rent-A-Cruise of Paris Landing, Rt. 3, Paris Landing, Buchanan, 38222. (901) 642-4798.

Birdsong Dock, Tennessee-Kentucky Lake, Camden, 38320.

The Maywalds, Rt. 1, Box, 55, Celina, 38551. (615) 243-2211.

Dale Hollow Dock, Rt. 1, Dale Hollow Lake, 38551.

Lake Richland Resort, Rt. 1, Dayton, 37321.

Loret Marina, Highway 58 N., Harrison, 37341.

Hixon Marina, Hixon, 37343. (615) 877-6621.

Horse Creek Marina, Horse Creek, 38551. (615) 243-2125.

U-Skipper Houseboat Rentals, Kilgore Flat Hollow Boat Dock, LaFollette, 37766. (615) 562-8314.

Norris Aqua Center, Box N, Norris, 37828. (615) 494-9992.

Perryville Marina, Box 97, Perryville, 38364.

Hurricane Dock Resort, Rt. 2, Silver Point, 38582. (615) 365-5146.

Thief Neck Park Marina, Rt. 2, Box 502, Rockwood, 37854. (615) 354-2974.

VIRGINIA

Hampton Roads Marina, Marina & Ivy Home Rds., Hampton, 23369.

Saunders Marina, Rt. 1, Huddleston, 24104.

Atlantic Leasing, 1829 Laskin Rd., Virginia Beach, 23451.

WEST VIRGINIA

Les Williams Marina, Sutton, 26601.

13

Rentals in the Midwest, Far West, and Beyond

NORTH CENTRAL REGION

ILLINOIS
Pirate's Cove Marina, Box 59, Carbondale, 62901.
Rent-A-Cruise of Illinois, 104 Warren Pl., DeKalb, 60115.
Adventurer Houseboat Rentals, 748 Deborah, Elgin, 60120.
Mississippi River Cruisers, Inc., Box 192, Elmhurst, 60126.
C&K Houseboat Rentals, 3513 Chestnut Dr., Hazelcrest, 60429.
Cruising Houseboats, Inc., 8250 N. Oriole, Niles, 60648.
Rent-A-Cruise of Peoria, Box 385, Peoria, 61601.
Quinsippi Houseboat Rental, 600 Adams, Quincy, 62301.
Rent-A-Cruise of Rock Island, 105 31st St., Rock Island, 61201.
Sunset Marina, Rock Island, 61201.
Twin Rivers Marina, Mile 283.25 on the Mississippi, Rockport, 62370.
Pitts Sport Store, 503 Main St., Savanna 61074.
Savanna River Cruises, Box 231, Savanna, 61074.
Starved Rock Marina, Box 106, Utica, 61373.

INDIANA
Coppers Marina, Green Blvd., U.S. Highway 50, Aurora, 47001.
U-Skipper of Lake Monroe, Four Winds Marina, Box 428, Bloomington, 47401.
Rent-A-Cruise of Monroe Lake, Box 256, Columbus, 47201.
Davy Jones Cruise Lines, Box 576, Jeffersonville, 47130.
Madison Marina, Vaughn Dr. and Central Ave., Madison, 47250. (812) 265-2256.

Tell City Marina, Sunset Park, Tell City, 47586.
Rent-A-Cruise of Evansville, Box 462, Vincennes, 47591.

I O W A
Great River Boating Co., Box 212, Clinton, 52732.
Mississippi Rent-A-Cruise, Rt. 1, Box 36, Clinton, 52732. (319) 243-1104.
United Rent-All, 9th St. at White, Dubuque, 52001. (319) 583-2112.
S & S Houseboat Rentals, 100 Harbor Dr., Lansing, 52151.
Houseboat Haven, Div. McGregor Development, McGregor, 52157.

K E N T U C K Y
Grider Hill Boat Dock, Hy. 734, Albany, 42602. (606) 387-5501.
Gordon's Dock, RFD #5, Benton, 42025. (502) 354-8157.
Holliday Cruises, Port Prizer Point, Rt. 4, Cadiz, 42211. (502) 522-3762.
Hendricks Creek Resort, (Dale Hollow Lake) Box 2107, North Canton, Ohio 44720. (216) 854-3523.
Anderson & Son Marine, Rt. 2-U.S. Hwy. 62W, Elizabethtown, 42701. (502) 765-5671.
Moore's Marina, Gilbertsville, 42044. (502) 362-4356.
Port Ken-Bar, Box 162, Grand Rivers, 42045. (502) 369-9972.
Christian's Marina, Clay's Ferry, Rt. 7, Lexington, 40505. (606) 266-4314.
Lexington Outdoor Marine, 175 New Circle Rd., N.E. Lexington, 40505.
Fairview Boat Harbor, 4001 Upper River Rd., Louisville, 40207.
Leisure Cruise, 309 North 4th St., Murray, 42071. (502) 753-3104.
Lack's Chris-Craft Sales, Box 367, 3300 S. Beltline, Paducah, 42001.
Hull Marine, Prestonburg, 41653. (606) 478-4483.
Alligator Dock, Rt. 5, Box 261, Russell Springs, 42642.

M I C H I G A N
Tower Marina, Box 114, Douglas, 49406. (616) 857-2682.
Sunset Marina, 1784 N. Channel Dr., Harsen's Island, 48028.
Toledo Beach Marina, S. Otter Creek Rd., Monroe, 48161. (313) 241-0823.
Rent-A-Cruise of Lake St. Clair, Hide-A-Way Harbor, 45044 Jefferson, Mt. Clemens, 48043.
Wyandotte Boat Rentals, 471 Biddle Ave., Wyandotte, 48192. (313) 284-0400.

M I N N E S O T A
Wilderness Holidays, Blue Earth, 56013.
"Voyaguaire" Houseboats, Rt. 2, Crane Lake, 55725. (218) 993-2105.
Lazy U Campground, Garfield, 56332.
Northernaire Floating Lodge, Rainy Lake, International Falls, 56649.
Northside Mercury, 800 W. Broadway, Minneapolis, 55411. (612) 521-7674.
Minnesota/Voyageur Houseboats, Box 1515, Orr, 55771.
Hiawatha Valley Cruises, Wabasha, 55981. (612) 565-4868.
Fisher's Houseboats, Box 98, Walker, 56484. (218) 547-1162.

Willis Soutbine, Watervelle, 56096.
Minnetonka Boat Works, Wayzata, 55391.

OHIO
Holiday Houseboat Rentals, 4333 River Rd., Cincinnati, 45204. (512) 921-4444.
Rick Drever, 10654 Deerfield Rd., Cincinnati, 45242. (513) 891-4558.
Suburban Rent-A-Cruise, 5963 Harrison, Cincinnati, 45200.
Captain's Cove Rent-A-Cruise, Captain's Cove Marina, Box 95, Franklin Furnace, 45629.
Rent-A-Cruise of Buckeye Lake, Millersport Marina, Box 415, Millersport, 43046.
Rent-A-Cruise of Sandusky, 703 E. Water St., Sandusky, 44870.
Bond's Hardware Marine Sales, 3896 Central Ave., Shadyside, 43947.
Happy Birthday, Inc., 334 Scioto St., Urbana, 43078.

WISCONSIN
Cruising Houseboats, Inc., Alma Marine, 8250 N. Oriole, Niles, Illinois, 60648.
Hiawatha Valley, Box 125, Alma, 54610. (608) 248-2325.
Holiday Harbor, Rt. 3-F, Eagle River, 54521.
Party Doll Fleet, Rt. 2, Fremont, 54940. (414) 446-2224.
Houseboat Rentals, Rt. 1, Hudson, 54016. (612) 436-7386.
Holiday Vacation Cruises, 1933 Rose St., LaCrosse, 54601.
Upper Mississippi Cruises, 2039 Rose St., LaCrosse, 54601.
Clark & Lund Boat Co., W. 4th & Michigan, Box 255, Oshkosh, 54901.

SOUTH CENTRAL REGION

ARKANSAS
Rent-A-Cruise of Hot Springs, Box 5408, Little Rock, 72205. (501) 663-7301.
Rent-A-Cruise of Lake Ouachita, Mountain Harbor Resort, Hwy. 270 RFD, Mt. Ida, 71957.
Rocky Branch Marina, Rt. 5, Beaver Lake, Rogers, 72756.
Holiday Afloat, Ramada Inn Marina, Russellville, 72801. (501) 968-1450.

KANSAS
Campbell's Marina, Wilson Lake RFD, Wilson, 67490. (913) 658-4392.

LOUISIANA
Rent-A-Cruise of New Orleans, Box 1428, Chalmette, 70043.

MISSOURI
Rent-A-Cruise of Lake of the Ozarks, Page Boat Yard, State Rd. P., Gravois, 65037. (314) 372-6801.
Rent-A-Cruise of Holiday Beach, Lake Pomme de Terre, Hermitage, 65668.

Water House Rentals, Table Rock Lake Road, Kimberling City, 65686. (417) 739-4365.

Drake Marine, Rt. 5-F, Sunrise Beach, Lake of the Ozarks, 65079. (314) 374-5231.

Water House Rentals, Lake Rd., 13-50-1, Reed Springs, 65737. (417) 739-4365.

Rent-A-Cruise of Table Rock Lake, 2275 E. Sunshine St., Springfield, 65804.

Rent-A-Cruise of America, Box 3558, Springfield, 65804. (For rentals throughout the U.S. call toll free 800 641-7343.)

House of Martin Sales, Box 9111, St. Louis, 63117. (314) 725-6320.

Rent-A-Cruise of St. Louis, 5950 Delmar Blvd., St. Louis, 63112. (314) 727-3616.

NEBRASKA
Dave Charters, Ponca, 68770. (402) 765-2511.

OKLAHOMA
Rent-A-Cruise of Lake Keystone, Pt. DX, Box 166, Cleveland, 74020.

TEXAS
U-Skipper Houseboat Rentals, Don Marsh Marina, Austin, 78710. (512) 266-1150.

C. B. Delhomme, Inc., 2101, Leland, Houston, 77000.

NORTHWESTERN REGION

IDAHO
Priest Lake Marina, Rt. 5, Priest Lake, 83856.

Sun-up Bay Resort, Lake Coeur d'Alene, Worley, 83876. (208) 664-6810.

OREGON
Rent-A-Cruise of Portland, Donaldson Marina, 3501 N.E. Marine Dr., Portland, 97211. (503) 288-6169.

UTAH
Aqua-Cruz, Halls Crossing Marina, Blanding, 84511.

Aqua-Cruz, 532 Kensington, Fillmore, California, 93015. (805) 524-3501.

Bullfrog Marina, 231 E. 4th St. S., Salt Lake City, 84111.

WASHINGTON
Recreational Facilities, Box 726, Anacortes, 98221. (206) 695-0920.

Beacon Marine, Pasco Port Dock, Box 113, Pasco and Wallula Junction, 99301. (509) 547-3962.

ABC Charters, 8126 224th S.W., Edmunds, Seattle, 98106. (206) 283-6160.

Recreational Facilities, 115 1st St., Washougal, 98671.

SOUTHWESTERN REGION

ARIZONA

Arizona Boat-homes, Box 1781, Page, 86040, or 4737 N. 21st Ave., Phoenix, 85015.

Canyon Tours, Inc., Waheap Marina, Box 1597, Page, 86040.

CALIFORNIA

S & H Boat Yard, Rt. 1, Box 514-E., Antioch, 94509.

Bridge Marina Houseboats, Rt. 1, Box 524, Antioch, 94509.

Carter's Deluxe Houseboat Rentals, Box 209, Bethel Island, 94511.

Delta-Cruz Houseboat Rentals, San Mound Blvd., Box 392, Bethel Island, 94511.

Aqua-Cruz, 532 Kensington Dr., Fillmore, 93015.

Fran's Houseboat Rentals, B & W Boat Harbor, Box 52-B, Isleton, 95641. (916) 777-6533.

Van Vee's Houseboat Rentals, Rt. 1, Box 61-C, Isleton, 95641.

Cast-Away Houseboat Rentals, Box 486, Lakeport, 95453.

Ralph L. Moore Yacht Broker, 6400 E. Pacific Coast Hwy., Long Beach, 90803.

Rent-A-Cruise, 5878 Gaviota Ave., Long Beach, 90805. (213) 422-4376.

International Houseboats, 721 N. LaBrea Ave., Los Angeles, 90038. (213) 933-5586.

Rent-A-Cruise of Lower Colorado River, Park Moabi Marina, Needles, 92363.

Charter Central, Box 1138, Newport Beach, 92663.

Lilly's Holiday Marine, 2200 W. Coast Hwy., Newport Beach, 92660.

Holiday Harbor, Shasta Lake, Box 112, O'Brien, 96970. (916) 238-2412.

Cast-away Houseboat Rental, Box 384, Oroville, 95464. (707) 274-1365.

Aqua Flowtels, Box 275, Redding, 96001. (916) 275-3773.

Holiday Floatels, Box 336, Redding, 96001. (916) 246-1283.

Jones Valley Marina, 8800 Bear Mountain Rd., Redding, 96001.

Westaire Floatels, Box 2358-S, Redding, 96001. (916) 241-6593.

Havalark, Box 5386, San Jose, 94150.

Holiday Floatels Delta, Box 8771, Stockton, 95204.

Tiki Laguna, 12988 W. McDonald Rd., Stockton, 95206.

Turner Cut Resort, 12888 W. McDonald Rd., Stockton, 95206.

Uncle Bobbie's Houseboat Haven, 11550 W. 8-Mile Rd., Stockton, 95207.

Ladd's Stockton Marina, Brookside Rd., Box 1385, Stockton, 95201.

American Floatels, Box 4581, Walnut Grove, 94596.

Withmore's Holiday Flotels Trinity, Weaverville, 96093.

HAWAII

Housecruisers Hawaii, Box 905, Kailua-Kona, 96740.

BEYOND OUR BORDERS

C A N A D A

The popularity of houseboating extends to many vacation areas beyond our borders. In Canada, the range of experiences includes cruising wilderness lakes (primarily for fishing and hunting) to the historic St. Lawrence Voyageurs Seaway with its shoreline of sweeping vistas, old ports, and quaint towns. From Sicamous, British Columbia, touted as the "Houseboat Capitol of Canada," across the sweep of provinces to the Atlantic Ocean, you'll find what you're looking for. Further information can be obtained from the Department of Tourism, of the province of your choice.

C A R I B B E A N

The Caribbean Sea offers the houseboater a different type of cruise, one set in crystal clear waters, abounding in pirate lore and visual beauty. You'll enjoy the native's tempo of living and discover on your own tropical vegetation, exotic flowers and birds, soft winds, lazy palms, and inviting beaches. Cruising the Caribbean, there's no dinner jacket formality as you experience the role of swashbuckler, beachcomber, Long John Silver, or jet-setter. It is a way of life we all yearn for—if but for a short blessed respite from daily toil. More information from:

Carib Explorers, 375 Park Ave., New York, New York 10022. (212) 758-8365.

Seafari, Ltd., Box 30, Freeport, Long Island, New York 11520. (516) 623-1010.

Virgin Islands, HBI, Mariners Ltd., 1740 Broadway, New York, New York. (212) 765-5630.

E U R O P E

Popular vacation areas in Europe are more and more seeing the houseboat offering a floating home in some preferred locale or cruising the historical and picturesque countryside. Along the canals and rivers the houseboater can stop at quaint villages, eat in native inns, or hike along the banks and picnic under the trees. Consult your local travel agency for the country of your choice.

There are approximately 19,000 navigable waterways in the United States. Approximately 80 percent are indicated on this chart. The other significant houseboat waters are along the Pacific Coast, Hawaii, and Alaska. (Courtesy U.S. Corps of Engineers)

14

Houseboating Waters
in the Northeast

There are many sources of information on local and distant waters available to the houseboater. Brochures, booklets, charts, and similar materials are here listed, locating marinas, launching ramps, and fishing waters, along with regional safety and navigation regulations and other pertinent information, free unless otherwise stated. (Area indices cover four chapters.)

This compendium of houseboating waters, organized by regions in the U.S., is taken largely from *Sources of Waterway Information*, by the Outboard Boating Club of America, 401 N. Michigan Ave., Chicago, Illinois 60611.

NATIONAL SOURCES

Pier 66 Franchised Marina Directory lists the bodies of water where Pier 66 Franchised Marinas can be found, state by state, indicating facilities and services available.

In addition to the above directory the Phillips Petroleum Company publishes a series of coastwide cruising guides, which indicate true compass courses and distances for popular cruises between important harbors, illustrate aids to navigation on navigable waters and storm signals, and list the frequencies of principal radio broadcast stations in the area. Write: Phillips Petroleum Co., Bartlesville, Oklahoma 74004.

Mobil Safety Afloat describes buoys and waterway markers, rules of the road, Coast Guard equipment requirements, lights required after dark, emergency drills, safe fueling procedures, distress signals, and availability of information on navigation, piloting, radio weather reporting, public instruction courses. Write: Mobil Oil Corp., Marine Retail Department, 150 E. 42nd St., New York, New York 10017.

"Your Texaco Cruise Kit" contains cruising charts issued solely as guides to yachtsmen and not intended for navigation purposes. Locates authorized Texaco marine service stations. Write: Texaco Waterways Service, 135 E. 42nd St., New York, New York 10017.

NORTHEASTERN AREA

Waterway Guide offers detailed description of marinas along the East Coast. Write Waterway Guide, 238 West St., Annapolis, Maryland 21401 ($3 each plus 60¢ postage).

Boating Almanac comes in four volumes with complete descriptions of marine facilities on tidal waters. Each marina, yard, yacht club, and fishing station is pinpointed on reproductions of official government charts. Included are tide and current tables and charts, tables of distance between harbors, tables of sun and moon rising and setting.

Volume 1 covers Canadian border to Rhode Island and Massachusetts border; Volume 2, Massachusetts border to and including Long Island, New York City, and Connecticut; Volume 3, Canadian border at Lake Champlain, Hudson River, and all of New Jersey; Volume 4, all of Chesapeake Bay and its tributaries and all of the Atlantic shoreline of Maryland and Delaware. Write: G. W. Bromley & Co., 325 Spring St., New York, New York 10013. ($2 each, plus 75¢ postage.)

Mobil Cruising Guide No. 2 offers a waterway map of Montreal, Canada to Key West, Florida, including Hudson River, New Jersey Coast, Delaware and Chesapeake Bays. Write Mobil Oil (see above).

CONNECTICUT
Directory of Marinas and Yacht Club lists marinas and clubs and the facilities and services they offer. It is divided into sections according to location. Write Connecticut Development Commission, P.O. Box 865, State Office Bldg., Hartford, Connecticut 06115.

MAINE
Maine Boat Facilities and Access Sites is an inventory of public facilities on tidewaters and inland waters of Maine, indicating where there are launching fees, and some of the services available at the facilities. Write Maine State Park & Recreation Commission, Division of Waterways, State Office Bldg., Augusta, Maine 04330.

Recreation Opportunities at Hydroelectric Projects Licensed by the Federal Power Commission is a booklet showing where recreational facilities and activities exist at FPC-licensed hydroelectric power projects in Northeastern United States. Write: Federal Power Commission, 65 Duane St., New York, New York 10007.

MARYLAND

Maryland Sport Fishing Guide contains maps locating popular fishing areas and launching sites. Write: Department of Fish & Wildlife Administration, State Office Bldg., Annapolis, Maryland 21404.

For *Recreation Opportunities at Hydroelectric Projects* . . . see entry under Maine.

MASSACHUSETTS

"Access to Massachusetts Public Waters," an article in March-April 1970 *Massachusetts Wildlife*, describes public access program and lists sites constructed by the Massachusetts Access Board. Write: Department of Natural Resources, Public Access Rd., State Office Bldg., Government Center, 100 Cambridge St., Boston, Massachusetts 02202.

Sportsman's Guide to Cape Cod gives access locations and saltwater launching facilities. Write: Cape Cod Chamber of Commerce, S.G. 1, Hyannis, Massachusetts 02601.

No formal brochure is available, but for a listing of the names and locations of public launching ramps on coastal and inland fresh waters, write: Department of Public Safety, Division of Marine & Recreational Vehicles, 64 Causeway St., Boston, Massachusetts 02114.

For *Recreation Opportunities at Hydroelectric Projects* . . . see entry under Maine.

NEW HAMPSHIRE

New Hampshire Public Water Bodies and Public Access Points, Report #4 gives public access points on the state's public water bodies. It is based on field surveys in planning how to cope with projected recreational demand. Write: State of New Hampshire, Department of Safety, Division of Safety Services, Concord, New Hampshire 03301.

New Hampshire Boating Guide locates public launching sites and privately owned marina facilities and briefs you on New Hampshire boating laws and regulations. Write same agency as above.

NEW YORK

"*The Northwest Passage Cruise'n Chart*" gives complete marine facility index plus a listing of historic sites and points of interest along the entire water route from New York City to the Canadian border. Write: State of New York, Office of Parks & Recreation, Division of Marine & Recreational Vehicles, South Mall, Albany, New York 12223.

"Listing of Existing Pump-out Facilities, as of November 1969" locates state pump-out stations for boats with waste retention systems. Write same agency as above.

A *Great Inland Waterway Barge Canal System* gives an introduction to the 524-mile toll-free system of canals and canalized lakes with navigation data, their history, and information about their value to pleasure boating. Write: New York State, Department of Transportation, Waterways Maintenance Subdivision, State Campus, Bldg. #5, Albany, New York 12226.

Cruising the Canal System gives a few basic rules and regulations for all boaters, plus description of four cruising routes. Write same agency as above.

"Map of Barge Canal System and Connecting Waterways" is a detailed map of canal system, lock numbers, and elevations. Write same agency as above.

"Public Marinas in Suffolk County" lists public and private marinas and yacht clubs in Suffolk County, New York. Write: Suffolk County Planning Department, Veterans Memorial Highway, Hauppauge, New York 11787.

"Boating Facilities-1972" is a map of Dutchess County showing public and commercial boating facilities and a related chart. Write: Dutchess County Department of Planning, 47 Cannon St., Poughkeepsie, New York 12601.

When traveling the canals of New York, especially the Erie, you have the interesting experience of cruising the canal and actually looking down on the countryside, a patchwork quilt of farmlands, for in many sectors the canal is higher than the land around it. The Erie Canal offers interesting towns that welcome houseboaters with excellent facilities and such summer events as boat races, beauty pageants, carnivals, and so on. Going from New York City to Niagara Falls via the Hudson River and Erie Canal is an interesting historical cruise, as is the alternate Lake Champlain route.

The Finger Lakes offer connecting waters with hundreds of miles of shoreline through the locks at Seneca Falls or northward on to Lake Ontario and the Thousand Island wonderland.

St. Johnsville, located halfway between the Hudson River and Lake Oneida on the Erie section of the barge canal, has a municipal marina with launching ramps and docking facilities. Information is available from Village of St. Johnsville, St. Johnsville, New York 13452.

PENNSYLVANIA

"Boating Guide to Pennsylvania Waters" is a comprehensive list of boating waters throughout Pennsylvania. Shown are listings of boating waters and access to these waters. Write: Waterways Division, Fish Commission, P.O. Box 1673, Harrisburg, Pennsylvania 17120.

For *Recreation Opportunities at Hydroelectric Projects Licensed by the Federal Power Commission*, see entry under Maine.

RHODE ISLAND

Boating in Rhode Island lists all Rhode Island marinas with their services and facilities; small boat launching ramps, fresh and salt water; boat builders and yards; electronics, radio repair and compass adjustment services; marine architects, boating laws, boats for charter. Write: Tourist Promotion Division, Rhode Island Development Council, Roger Williams Bldg., Providence, Rhode Island 02908.

"Rhode Island Tourist Guide" is a calendar of events in boating, fishing, surfing, and other recreational activities: what to see, where to stay, and what to do. Write same agency as above.

"Rhode Island Recreation Map" shows public boat launching sites. Includes a facilities chart for the state's Island Park System. Write same agency as above.

The northeast section of our country is the historical center of boating and leads in boat sales and participation. (Kierkaker Mercury Photo)

VERMONT

Laws and Regulations Governing Use and Registration of Motorboats states motorboat law, rules and regulations, and safety hints on motorboating. Write: State of Vermont, Department of Public Safety, Marine Division, Montpelier, Vermont 05602.

Vermont Guide to Fishing contains a detailed map of prime areas for fishing. Also locates marinas, boat landings, boat rentals, and camping areas. Write same agency as above.

"State of Vermont—Rules and Regulations for Use of Recreational Areas" lists regulations for use of state's forests and parks. Reverse side is map of Burton Island State Park on Lake Champlain, which facility includes a boat ramp, marina, cabins, sanitation facilities, campgrounds, and boat sanitary dump station. Write: State of Vermont, Department of Forests and Parks, Montpelier, Vermont 05602.

The northeast section of our country represents the traditional center of boating. Boat sales and participation in these states lead all the others. Little wonder. The Atlantic Coast is lined with continuous waterways. They provide a protected boating route along most of the coastline from Massachusetts to Florida. The Intercoastal Waterway cuts through marshes and swamps, down rivers, through bayous, estuaries, and other bodies of water. Along the route it is possible for the houseboater to enjoy almost every imaginable type of water experience. Harbors, marinas, and other services are available at intervals along the route; so it's just a matter of following the charts and keeping an eye on the weather.

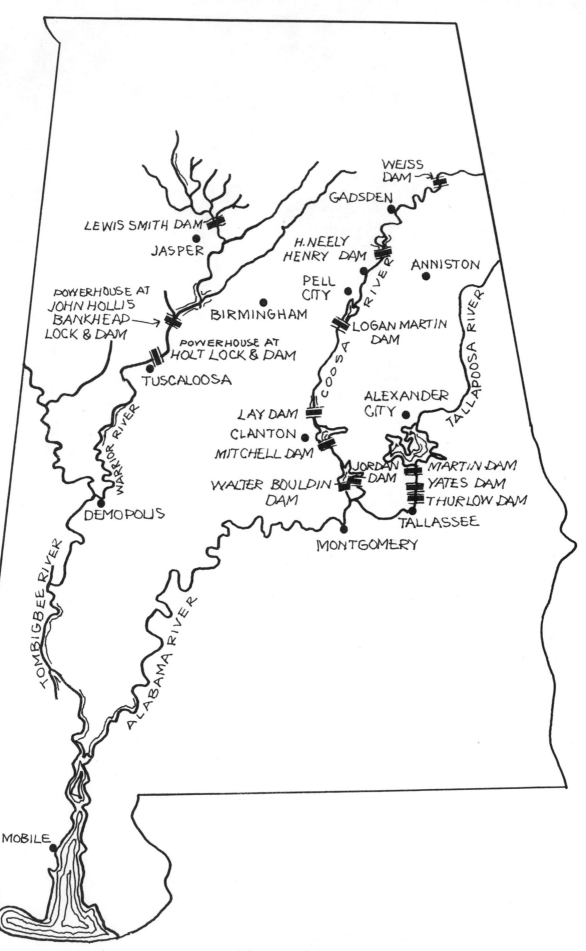

Alabama rivers, their locks and dams

15

Southeastern Area
of Participation

ALABAMA

"Lakes of the Mobile District" includes several maps showing availability of facilities at reservoir projects of the Mobile District on the Black Warrior and Tombigbee Rivers in western Alabama and on the Chattahoochee River boundary of Alabama and Georgia. Write U.S. Army Corps of Engineers, Mobile District, P.O. Box 2288, Mobile, Alabama 36628.

"Alabama Power Co. Lakes Create 145,000 Acres of Fun" describes various power company lakes and recreational facilities available. Write: Alabama Department of Conservation, Information and Education Section, Administrative Bldg., Montgomery, Alabama 36104.

FLORIDA

Florida, the sunshine state, offers the houseboater both the Atlantic and Gulf of Mexico coasts, estuaries, bays, inland lakes, and rivers— endless waters to cruise. The shallow waters and reefs of the Gulf do not pose a problem for the houseboater (with his low draft), and, weather permitting, he can stay asea for weeks. The Florida Keys offer a tropical paradise of South Sea advantages. The vast inland Lake Okeechobee, St. Johns River, and hundreds of ideal waters are best explored, cruised, and fished from the houseboat.

Florida Boating is a handy 93-page illustrated guide to cruising Florida waterways, including a directory of marinas and boat launching ramps, a briefing on Florida boating laws, safety tips, navigation and weather data, and suggestions on where to go in the sunshine state. Write: Bureau of Education & Information, Department of Natural Resources, Larson Bldg., Tallahassee, Florida 32304.

"Dade County Park & Recreation Department" gives information on five modern marinas accommodating more than 400 boats. Dockage, free ramps, parking, along with fuel, bait, tackle, and supplies are available. There are also boat hoists and dry storage facilities. Write: Public Information Section, Metro Dade County Park & Recreation Department, 50 S.W. 32nd Rd., Miami, Florida 33129.

"Elliott Key Park" describes a 90-acre public recreation area 20 miles southeast of Miami accessible only by boat, featuring a 62-boat harbor, an overnight camping area, and a boating supplies store. Write same agency as above.

"Lists of Marinas and Boat Ramps in Florida" are three separate compilations of marinas and their location, boat ramps constructed by the Florida Game and Fresh Water Fish Commission and their location, and coastal launching facilities. Write: Florida Department of Natural Resources, Bureau of Education & Information, Rm. 664, Larson Bldg., Jacksonville, Florida 32201.

"Municipal Boat Launching Ramps" is a map indicating municipal launching ramps and their location in St. Petersburg. Write: Parks & Recreation Department, City of St. Petersburg, 1450-16th St., N., St. Petersburg, Florida 38804.

For *Recreation Opportunities at Hydroelectric Projects Licensed by the Federal Power Commission* see entry under Alabama.

Florida, with over 2,200 miles of tidal shoreline and with thousands of navigable lakes and rivers, offers unlimited opportunities for pleasant houseboat cruising, exciting exploring, and fishing. A brief overview of a few routes includes:

Atlantic Intercoastal Waterway goes from Fernandina to Miami, a distance of 349 miles. Completely protected, the waterway parallels the coast, and facilities for boat and crew are numerous. Miami to Key West, via Hawk Channel, is a buoyed passage between the outermost reefs and the Keys, usually a mile or two offshore.

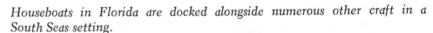

Houseboats in Florida are docked alongside numerous other craft in a South Seas setting.

Gulf Intracoastal Waterway, Pensacola to Carrabelle, traverses a distance of 230 miles, through protected harbors and inland canal. Carrabelle to St. Marks Light is 30 miles, with a channel depth limited to 3 feet. Anclote to Ft. Myers totals 130 miles, with 9-foot depth through protected harbors and an inland canal.

Okeechobee Waterway from St. Lucie Inlet across the state to Ft. Myers, totals 135 miles: 38 on the St. Lucie Canal, 40 across Lake Okeechobee, and 57 on the Caloosahatchee River. Four locks are in operation on the St. Lucie Canal.

St. John's River, from Mayport to Sanford and Jacksonville to Palatka and Welaka, offers a channel depth of 3 to 13 feet, and day and night markers are maintained.

Kissimmee Waterway from the town of Kissimmee across Lakes Tohopekaliga, Cypress, Hatchineha, and Kissimmee, down river to Lake Okeechobee goes a distance of 97 miles. This cruise passes through one of the least explored areas of the state, and while sections of it are open to boatmen at all times, it is advisable to check locally for directions and the condition of the waterway in its entirety.

Suwannee River from the town of Suwannee on the Gulf to Bradford is 70 miles, and the river channel is deep and wide. In Manatee Springs State Park, 20 miles from the Gulf, facilities are available for overnight camping, swimming, and picnicking. From the mouth of the river to Cedar Key is 15 miles, with a marked daytime channel maintained through East Pass.

Perhaps you'll wish to time your Gulf cruise to coincide with the "Fiesta of Five Flags" at Pensacola, Art Fair at Cedar Key, regatta at St. Petersburg, or a wild boar barbecue someplace down the coast.

In the St. Petersburg-Tampa area the houseboat fleet continues to grow each year. It is possible, though occasionally not practical, to houseboat every day of the year. Even if you eliminated a month from the helm, there would still be more boating weather left over than any other state can claim.

Experienced skippers with seaworthy houseboats can launch at one of the Gulf's numerous marinas and head out for in-shore trolling to catch king and Spanish mackerel, bluefish, dolphin, bonito, speckled trout, jack crevalle, cobia and flounder.

U.S. Coast and Geodetic Survey publishes at least five different types of charts that would be helpful to boaters planning to use the coastal and inland waterways in Florida. For charts and prices write: Director, U.S. Coast & Geodetic Survey, Environmental Science Services Administration, Rockville, Maryland 20852.

GEORGIA
Boating and Fishing in Georgia State Parks is a directory of State Parks indicating types of boats allowed and availability of boat launching ramps and docks. Write: Georgia Department of State Parks, 270 Washington St., S.W., Atlanta, Georgia 30334.

Georgia State Parks is a directory showing availability of boat ramps, docks, and rentals. Write same source as above.

"Welcome to Tobesofkee" is a location map and description of 1750-acre lake owned and operated by Bibb County. Write: Greater Macon Chamber of Commerce, P.O. Box 169, Macon, Georgia 31202.

"Hartwell and Clark Hill Dams and Reservoirs" includes map of recreational areas and available facilities and project data for these two impoundments on the Georgia-South Carolina border. Write: U.S. Army Corps of Engineers, Savannah District, Savannah, Georgia 31402.

"Buford Dam and Lake Lanier, Allatoona Reservoir, Lake Seminole, George Lock and Dam" are maps of recreational areas and available facilities at reservoir projects of the Mobile District in Georgia with project data. Write: U.S. Corps of Engineers, Mobile District, P.O. Box 2288, Mobile, Alabama 36601.

Booklet, *Recreation Opportunities at Hydroelectric Projects Licensed by the Federal Power Commission*, shows where recreational facilities and activities exist at FPC-licensed hydroelectric power projects in southeastern United States. Write Federal Power Commission, 730 Peachtree St., Atlanta, Georgia 30308.

MISSISSIPPI

Pleasure Boating in Mississippi describes recreational water areas in the state and the facilities available, with a digest of rules and regulations. Write: Mississippi Boat and Water Safety Commission, Room 403, Robert E. Lee Bldg., Jackson, Mississippi 39201.

"Okatibbee Reservoir" is a map of Engineer Corps impoundment on Okatibbee Creek showing summer operating pool and access roads. Reverse side shows public use regulations and rules. Write: U.S. Army Corps of Engineers, Mobile District, P.O. Box 2288, Mobile, Alabama 36601.

NORTH CAROLINA

Boat Access Areas, a book, is designed to help boaters more easily locate the free boating access areas operated throughout the state by the Wildlife Resources Commission. Include are coded maps, and indices to available fishery and recreational activities in each are given. Write: North Carolina Department of Natural and Economic Resources Commission, P.O. Box 2919, Raleigh, North Carolina 27611.

"Locks and Dams, Cape Fear River" offers information about three Corps of Engineers locks and dams on the Cape Fear River and the free recreational facilities offered in connection with them. Write: Corps of Engineers (Mobile District, above), or Reservoir Manager, John H. Kerr Dam & Reservoir, Rt. 1, Box 76, Boydon, Virginia 23917.

"John H. Kerr Dam & Reservoir Recreation Facilities" lists federal recreation areas operated by the Corps, indicating special recreational facilities. Write same source as above.

SOUTH CAROLINA

"South Carolina Boat Landings" indicates where the public may launch boats without paying for access. General locations of the public boat ramps are shown on state map. Specific information on each ramp

A sunset off Pensacola, Florida

can be obtained from maps on reverse side. Also shows rules of the road and illustrates Uniform Waterway Markers, storm signals, and distress signals. Write: South Carolina Wildlife Resources Department, Division of Boating, 15 Lockwood Blvd., Charleston, South Carolina 29401.

South Carolina Parks is a guide to recreational attractions and facilities at state parks, federal recreation areas in the state, and commercial campgrounds. A chart shows where the free launch ramps and boat rentals are. Write: South Carolina Department of Tourism, P.O. Box 1358, Columbia, South Carolina 29202.

For *Recreation Opportunities at Hydroelectric Projects Licensed by the Federal Power Commission*, see entry under Alabama.

TENNESSEE

"Tennessee Outdoors" is a map of the state pinpointing State Game and Fish Commission Wildlife management areas and lakes, and boating requirements. Write: Tennessee Conservation Department, Division of Tourist Information, 2611 West End Ave., Nashville, Tennessee 37203.

"Tennessee's Kentucky Lake," a map, details Kentucky Lake showing privately owned resorts and marinas and fishing opportunities. Write: Tennessee Kentucky Lake Association, Rt. 2, Buchanan, Tennessee 38222.

"Recreation on TVA Lakes" lists public and commercial boating facilities, their location by river mile, and the type of services and accommodations each provides. Write: Tennessee Valley Authority, 200 Haney Bldg., Chattanooga, Tennessee 37401, or Information Office, Tennessee Valley Authority, Knoxville, Tennessee 37902.

"Land Between the Lakes" describes facilities available within TVA's Land Between the Lakes area between Kentucky and Barkley Lake. Write same source as above.

"Index to Navigation Charts and Maps of TVA Reservoirs" lists prices for different scales and sizes and illustrates the type of information the maps provide. Write same source as above.

"Recreation Maps Tennessee Valley Lakes" show public access areas, commercial recreation areas, boat docks, launching sites, and access roads around the lakes. Write same source as above (up to two copies free).

"Ohio River and Tributaries, Small Boat Harbors, Ramps, Landings, etc." lists and locates by river mile public craft facilities and services available on tributaries of the Ohio River in the Nashville District of the Corps of Engineers. Write: U.S. Army Engineer District, Nashville, P.O. Box 1070, Nashville, Tennessee 37202 (price 50¢).

Tennessee River Navigation Charts is a bound two-color set of charts showing docks, mile points, navigation aids, safety harbors, and normal pool elevations from Paducah, Kentucky, to Knoxville, Tennessee. Write same source as above (price $2.50).

Cumberland River Navigation Charts offers same data as above from Ohio River to Carthage, Tennessee. Write same source as above (price $2.00).

The Tennessee Valley Authority has 36 reservoirs in seven states, with 11,000 miles of shoreline—a houseboater's paradise with many public parks, docks, and adequate launching facilities.

The TVA Recreation map of Norris Lake indicates public lands, state and county parks, and commercial marinas. It is bordered by the Cumberland Mountains, and the feeder Clinch River provides a clear-water stretch for houseboating. The lake's shoreline is replete with quiet coves, bays, and arms, which provide privacy for activities and overnight anchorage—either tying to a tree on shore or pulling up on the beach. Write: Tennessee Valley Lakes (Recreation Maps), 102-A Union Bldg., Knoxville, Tennessee 37902, or 110 Pound Bldg., Chattanooga, Tennessee 37401.

VIRGINIA

Guide to Virginia Marinas, Docks, and Railways is a county-by-county listing of privately owned and operated pleasure boating facilities, including depth of dock, low water, the number of berths, storage, in-out service, fuel available, and repairs. Also it contains illustration of Uniform Waterways Markers System. Write: Virginia Commission of Game & Inland Fisheries, P.O. Box 11104, Richmond, Virginia 23230.

Boating Access to Virginia Waters, a book, gives maps locating boaters' access points throughout the state. Write same source as above. "Phillpot Dam and Reservoir" map locates boat launching ramps and docks, access roads, and areas off limits to boating and water skiing. Lists boating and service facilities available at each recreation area. Write: U.S. Army Corps of Engineers, Wilmington District, P.O. Box 1890, Wilmington, North Carolina 28401, or Reservoir Manager, Phillpot Dam, Rt. 2, Box 140, Basset, Virginia 24055.

WEST VIRGINIA

"Ohio River and Tributaries" gives a detailed list of facilities and services for pleasure craft operators on the Ohio River and its tributaries in West Virginia and several other states. The list is revised annually. Write: U.S. Army Engineer, District of Huntington, P.O. Box 2127, Huntington, West Virginia 25721 (price 50¢).

Locking Through is a pamphlet to assure safety in using locks. Write same source as above.

16

Midwestern and South Central Areas' Potential for Houseboating

The Mississippi River is the Midwest's ocean. It touches eight states of the area and with its tributaries, quiet back-offs, and secluded coves, offers a most interesting houseboating experience. Many stretches of the river are wide enough to give the feeling of being on a large lake, for the Miss' is actually a series of deep pools formed by dams and locks. The backed-up waters form linear lakes that extend laterally over flat land to form quiet backwaters and bayous. The dams maintain depth for all types of craft to be able to cruise all the way to the Gulf of Mexico.

Commercial freighting is extensive on the Miss'. Powerful towboats, used exclusively on rivers and other protected waters, are capable of pushing barges carrying as much as 40,000 to 50,000 tons of cargo. The towboat uses the push-towing (over pull-towing) method on barges that are tied rigidly together by steel cables to form a single unit. The flat-bottomed towboat, with massive power, uses multiple rudders which afford maximum control for forward, backward, and flanking movements. Houseboaters cruising on commercial waterways must be ever-vigilant of the strings of barges being pushed by towboats.

The appeal of the Mississippi River was noted by Mark Twain, and today houseboaters can savor many of the sights and experiences he wrote about. Houseboat rentals are available all along the interesting and historic waterway. Cruising in a powered houseboat may not be like drifting on a raft, but there's a trace of Huck Finn adventure and more in viewing the backwaters, the remote fishing camps, river ports where vestiges of old riverboat days still cling, wild ducks feeding in the shallows, and the eagle soaring above.

Quimby's Harbor Guide (see entry under Wisconsin) lists all the harbors, marinas, and gas docks between Minneapolis and the mouth of the Ohio River. A guide of this nature is invaluable, as many of the sources for gas, service, and the like are not visible from the river, being located behind levees, off-channel, in sloughs, behind islands, or up inlets. Guides containing the above type of information are more valuable than navigation charts, for within the confined banks of a river there's little margin for navigation error. The guide is updated annually.

ILLINOIS

"Illinois Rivers Facilities Map" pinpoints boating facilities on the Mississippi, Illinois, Ohio, and Wabash Rivers in the state and shows service facilities available at each site. Write: State of Illinois, Department of Conservation, 102 State Office Bldg., Springfield, Illinois 62706.

U.S. Lake Survey Chart Catalog of the Great Lakes and Connecting Waters includes map showing segments of the Great Lakes covered by different navigation charts prepared by the U.S. Lake Survey and a list of the chart numbers and localities for your convenience in ordering. Write: U.S. Department of Commerce, National Ocean Survey, Lake Survey Center, 630 Federal Bldg., Detroit Michigan 48226.

"Crab Orchard National Wildlife Refuge" describes boating opportunities at refuge's lakes. Map locates access roads, boat ramps, marinas, and so on. Write: Project Manager, Crab Orchard National Wildlife Refuge, P.O. Box J, Carterville, Illinois 62918.

"Rockford Park District Doorway to Recreation" is a list of facilities provided by the Park District for launching boats on the Rock River. Write: Rockford Park District, 1401 N. 2nd St., Rockford, Illinois 61107.

Recreation Opportunities at Hydroelectric Projects Licensed by the Federal Power Commission, a booklet, shows where recreational fa-

The fortress-like palisades on the banks of the Mississippi River offer this Cruis-Ader crew a visual treat and respite from the main channel.

W I S C O N S I N

1ST PRESBYTERIAN CHURCH
GRANT'S HOME
MARKET HOUSE
DE SOTO HOTEL
ST. MICHEAL'S CHURCH

E. DUBUQUE

GALENA
APPLE RIVER
CANYON ST. PK.
LAKE LE-AQUA-NA ST. PK.
ROCKFORD

SCENIC RIDGE RD.
CHESTNUT HILL SKIING
LOCK AND DAM NO. 12
BOAT MARINA
Hanover
WHISTLING WINGS
MISS. PALISADES ST. PK.
Savanna
MT. CARROLL
SHIMER COLLEGE

ILLINOIS YOUTH CAMP
SAVANNA BOAT HARBOR
WATERMELON CAPITOL OF ILL.
XMAS TREE FORESTS
TOMATO & CUCUMBER CENTER
Thomson
Fulton
OLD MILL DAM
MORRISON
STERLING
SINNISSIPPI LAKE & CANAL
Albany
ROCK FALLS
ERIE LAKE
CAPT. HANK'S SAW MILL
INDIAN MOUNDS
BOAT MARINA
PROPHETSTOWN ST. PK.

CHICAGO

MICHIGAN

LEGEND
TEMPORARY AND PERMANENT MARKING OF THE
GREAT RIVER ROAD IN ILLINOIS

PERMANENT LOCATION
TEMPORARY LOCATION
RECOMMENDED FUTURE
LOCATION
INTERSTATE ROUTE

BLACK HAWK ST. PK.

LOCK AND DAM NO. 13

LOCK AND DAM NO. 14

ROCK ISLAND

LOCK AND DAM NO. 15

ANDALUSIA

MUSCATINE

GENESEO
FISH HATCHERY

KEWANEE LAKE

RAPIDS CITY

HAMPTON

RIVER

80

O

NEW BOSTON

LOCK AND DAM NO. 17

KEITHSBURG

BISHOP HILL
STATE MEM.

MISSISSIPPI

74

MOLINE

EAST MOLINE

SILVIS

80

ROCK ISLAND

280

280

92

92

74

80

74

ST. MARY'S ACADEMY
JOSEPH SMITH HOMESTEAD
BRIGHAM YOUNG HOME
NAUVOO STATE PARK
LAND OF THE WEDDING
OF THE WINE & CHEESE

LOCK AND DAM NO. 18

OQUAWKA
OLD COURT HOUSE
COVERED BRIDGE

DEDICATED
SECTION OF
GREAT RIVER
ROAD

NAUVOO

LOCK AND
DAM NO. 19

COVERED BRIDGE

WARSAW

HAMILTON

FORT EDWARDS

MACOMB
WESTERN ILLINOIS
UNIVERSITY

67

270

270

65

70

GRANITE CITY

111

70

LOCK AND
DAM NO. 20

M

INDIAN MOUNDS PARK
LIME KILNS
ILLINOIS SOLDIERS & SAILORS HOME
LINCOLN-DOUGLAS DEBATE OCT. 13, 1858

LOCK AND
DAM NO. 21

QUINCY COLLEGE

QUINCY

SILOAM SPRINGS
STATE PARK

SPRINGFIELD

70

255

EAST ST. LOUIS

70

64

64

HANNIBAL

DEDICATED
SECTION OF
GREAT RIVER
ROAD

LOCK AND DAM NO. 22
LOCK AND DAM NO. 24

S

RIVER

HARDIN

CAHOKIA

CENTREVILLE

255

COLUMBIA

158

LOCK AND DAM NO. 25

PERE MARQUETTE ST. PK.
THE PRINCIPIA COLLEGE
LOVEJOY MEM.
LINCOLN-DOUGLAS DEBATE MARKER
S.I.U. CENTER
LEWIS & CLARK STATE MEMORIAL

GRAFTON
ELSAH

ALTON

DEDICATED SECTION OF
GREAT RIVER ROAD

LOCK AND DAM NO. 26
LOCK AND DAM NO. 27

CAHOKIA MOUNDS ST. PK.

EAST ST. LOUIS

CAHOKIA

GRAND MARAIS ST. PK.

O

COLUMBIA

VALMEYER

MISSISSIPPI

Great River Road Illinois

STATE OF ILLINOIS
ROUTE OF THE
GREAT RIVER ROAD

FORT CHARTRES ST. PK.
MODOCK ROCK SHELTER
FORT KASKASKIA ST. PK.
KASKASKIA ST. MEM.

PRAIRIE DU ROCHER

SOUTHERN
ILLINOIS
UNIVERSITY

CRAB ORCHARD LAKE

DEVILS KITCHEN LAKE

WABASH

CHESTER

ROCKWOOD

MURPHYSBORO

CARBONDALE

LAKE MURPHYSBORO ST. PK.

GIANT CITY ST. PK.
FERNE CLYFFE ST. PK.

UNION COUNTY
CONSERVATION AREA

LITTLE
GRASSY
LAKE

RIVER

U

57

BURNHAM ISLAND
CONSERVATION AREA

THEBES

OHIO

HORSESHOE LAKE
CONSERVATION AREA

CAIRO

KENTUCKY

FORT DEFIANCE ST. PK.
MAGNOLIA MANOR

Route of the Great River Road of the Illinois Mississippi Scenic Parkway cilities and activities exist at FPC-licensed hydroelectric power projects in North Central United States. Write: Federal Power Commission, 610 S. Canal St., Chicago, Illinois 60607.

INDIANA

Monroe Reservoir details the location of the reservoir, user fees, boat launching ramps, covered ramps, moorings, and rentals. There is a map of access roads, launching ramps, and checking station. Write: Monroe Reservoir, R.R. #3, Box 214, Bloomington, Indiana 47401.

"Mississinewa Reservoir" is a description of the reservoir, access roads, and boat ramps. Write: Mississinewa Reservoir, Rt. 1, Box 194, Peru Indiana 46970.

For U.S. *Survey Chart Catalog of the Great Lakes and Connecting Water* see entry under Illinois.

IOWA

"De Soto National Wildlife Refuge" is a map of refuge located on Iowa-Nebraska border, showing boat ramps, regulations, and so on. Write: Refuge Manager, De Soto National Wildlife Refuge, Missouri Valley, Iowa 51555.

For *Quimby's Harbor Guide* see entry under Wisconsin.

KENTUCKY

"Land between the Lakes" is a complete list of lake access areas on Kentucky Lake-Lake Barkley and a map that plots their locations along the shoreline. Write: Tennessee Valley Authority, P.O. Box 27, Golden Pond, Kentucky 42231.

"Recreation on TVA Lakes" gives recreation areas including boat docks and county and municipal parks that have docks, each area located by comparing its river mile designation with figures on map. Write: Information Office, Tennessee Valley Authority, Knoxville, Tennessee 37902.

"Ohio River and Tributaries, Small Boat harbors, Ramps, Landings, etc." is a detailed list of facilities and services for pleasure craft operators on the Ohio River and its tributaries in Kentucky and several other states. The list is revised annually. Write: U.S. Army Engineer District, P.O. Box 59, Louisville, Kentucky 40201 (price 50¢).

MICHIGAN

"Michigan Recreational Harbor Facilities" is both a list and map of recreational harbor facilities around the state's Great Lakes shorelines. Write: Department of Natural Resources, Waterway Division, Stevens T. Mason Bldg., Lansing, Michigan 48926.

Michigan Harbors Guide offers a visual cruise of Michigan's Great Lakes waters, with pictures and maps of the network harbors of refuge developed by the Waterways Division, so that no boater will ever be more than about 15 shore miles from a safe harbor. Write same source as above.

Michigan Boat Launching Directory is designed to aid users of trailer-borne boats in locating places to launch. It lists information concerning

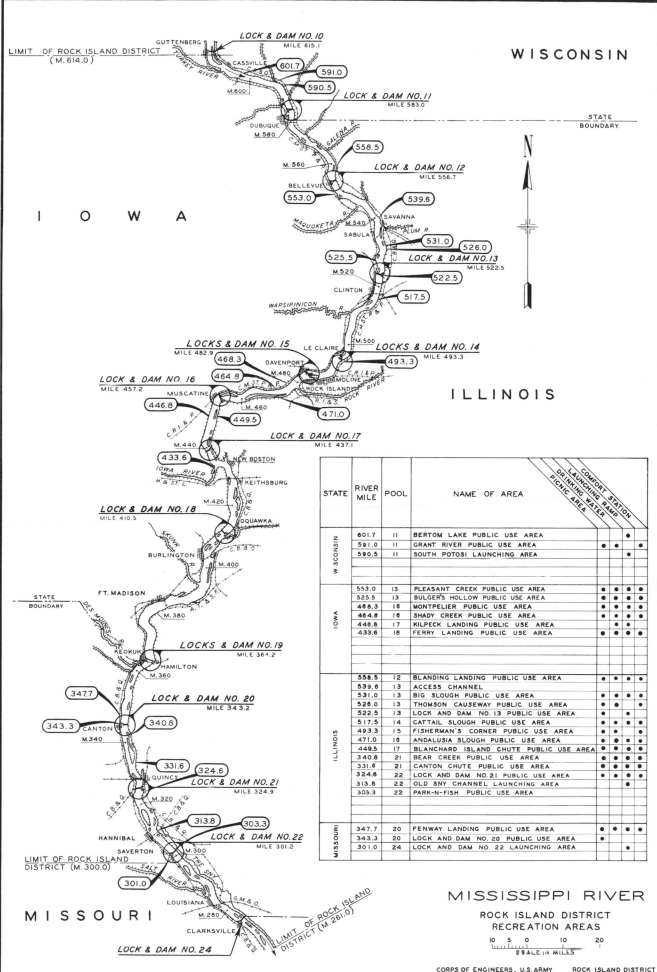

WISCONSIN

LIMIT OF ROCK ISLAND DISTRICT (M.614.0)

LOCK & DAM NO.10 MILE 615.1

GUTTENBERG
TURKEY RIVER
CASSVILLE
601.7
591.0
590.5

M.600

LOCK & DAM NO.11 MILE 583.0

DUBUQUE
M.580

STATE BOUNDARY

GALENA R.
M.560
558.5

LOCK & DAM NO.12 MILE 556.7

IOWA

BELLEVUE
553.0
539.6

MAQUOKETA R.
M.540
SAVANNA
PLUM R.
SABULA
531.0
526.0
525.5

LOCK & DAM NO.13 MILE 522.5

M.520
CLINTON
522.5
517.5

WAPSIPINICON R.
M.500
LE CLAIRE

LOCKS & DAM NO.15 MILE 482.9
468.3
464.8

DAVENPORT
M.480

LOCKS & DAM NO.14 MILE 493.3
493.3

LOCK & DAM NO.16 MILE 457.2

MUSCATINE
446.8
449.5
471.0

MOLINE
ROCK ISLAND
ROCK RIVER

ILLINOIS

M.460

LOCK & DAM NO.17 MILE 437.1
M.440
433.6

NEW BOSTON
IOWA RIVER
KEITHSBURG
M.420

LOCK & DAM NO.18 MILE 410.5

OQUAWKA

SKUNK R.
BURLINGTON
M.400

FT. MADISON
M.380

STATE BOUNDARY

DES MOINES R.
KEOKUK
LOCKS & DAM NO.19 MILE 364.2
HAMILTON
M.360

347.7
LOCK & DAM NO.20 MILE 343.2
343.3
CANTON
340.8
M.340

331.6
324.6
QUINCY
LOCK & DAM NO.21 MILE 324.9
M.320

313.8
303.3
LOCK & DAM NO.22 MILE 301.2

HANNIBAL
SAVERTON
M.300

LIMIT OF ROCK ISLAND DISTRICT (M.300.0)
SALT RIVER
THE SNY
301.0

LOUISIANA
M.280

LIMIT OF ROCK ISLAND DISTRICT (M.261.0)

MISSOURI

CLARKSVILLE

LOCK & DAM NO.24

STATE	RIVER MILE	POOL	NAME OF AREA	PICNIC AREA	DRINKING WATER	LAUNCHING RAMP	COMFORT STATION
WISCONSIN	601.7	11	BERTOM LAKE PUBLIC USE AREA			•	
	591.0	11	GRANT RIVER PUBLIC USE AREA	•	•	•	•
	590.5	11	SOUTH POTOSI LAUNCHING AREA			•	
IOWA	553.0	13	PLEASANT CREEK PUBLIC USE AREA	•	•	•	•
	525.5	13	BULGER'S HOLLOW PUBLIC USE AREA	•	•	•	•
	468.3	16	MONTPELIER PUBLIC USE AREA	•	•	•	•
	464.8	16	SHADY CREEK PUBLIC USE AREA	•	•	•	•
	446.8	17	KILPECK LANDING PUBLIC USE AREA	•	•	•	•
	433.6	18	FERRY LANDING PUBLIC USE AREA	•	•	•	•
ILLINOIS	558.5	12	BLANDING LANDING PUBLIC USE AREA	•	•	•	•
	539.6	13	ACCESS CHANNEL				
	531.0	13	BIG SLOUGH PUBLIC USE AREA	•	•	•	•
	526.0	13	THOMSON CAUSEWAY PUBLIC USE AREA	•	•	•	
	522.5	13	LOCK AND DAM NO.13 PUBLIC USE AREA	•		•	
	517.5	14	CATTAIL SLOUGH PUBLIC USE AREA	•	•	•	•
	493.3	15	FISHERMAN'S CORNER PUBLIC USE AREA	•	•	•	
	471.0	16	ANDALUSIA SLOUGH PUBLIC USE AREA	•	•	•	
	449.5	17	BLANCHARD ISLAND CHUTE PUBLIC USE AREA	•	•	•	•
	340.8	21	BEAR CREEK PUBLIC USE AREA	•	•	•	•
	331.6	21	CANTON CHUTE PUBLIC USE AREA	•	•	•	•
	324.6	22	LOCK AND DAM NO.21 PUBLIC USE AREA	•	•	•	
	313.8	22	OLD SNY CHANNEL LAUNCHING AREA			•	
	303.3	22	PARK-N-FISH PUBLIC USE AREA				
MISSOURI	347.7	20	FENWAY LANDING PUBLIC USE AREA	•	•	•	•
	343.3	20	LOCK AND DAM NO.20 PUBLIC USE AREA	•			
	301.0	24	LOCK AND DAM NO.22 LAUNCHING AREA			•	

MISSISSIPPI RIVER

ROCK ISLAND DISTRICT
RECREATION AREAS

10   5   0   10   20
SCALE IN MILES

CORPS OF ENGINEERS, U.S. ARMY   ROCK ISLAND DISTRICT
ROCK ISLAND, ILLINOIS   FEBRUARY 1968

each ramp and nearby facilities. Write: Department of Natural Resources, Marine Safety Division, Stevens T. Mason Bldg., Lansing, Michigan 48926.

"Huron-Clinton Metropolitan Authority Metropark Guide" is a map of facilities and water areas which serve the people of the counties of Livingston, Macomb, Oakland, Washtenaw, Wayne, and the city of Detroit. Write: Huron-Clinton Metropolitan Authority, 600 Woodward Ave., Detroit, Michigan 48226.

MINNESOTA

The far northern shore of Rainy Lake is truly a wilderness area, the waterway of the *voyageurs*, and the famed historic route of the fur traders. It is the back-yard playground of the citizenry of International Falls (Minnesota) and Fort Francis (Canada), and on holidays their entire populations, it seems, take to Rainy. It is a houseboater's dream, with 2,500 miles of shoreline, containing more than 1,800 islands. Where else can you, in season, catch limits of northern pike, walleye, small-mouth bass, deer, bear, grouse, and migratory fowl? The success ratio of better than average for deer hunters is claimed by Rainy Lake guides, for the many islands offer ideal cover for deer, and there is a minimum of hunters.

For *Recreation Opportunities at Hydroelectric Projects Licensed by the Federal Power Commission* see entry under Illinois.

For *Quimby's Harbor Guide* see entry under Wisconsin.

MISSOURI

"Missouri River Facilities" is no formal brochure but a list of small boat ramps, docks, and marinas along the Missouri and Mississippi rivers, avilable on request. Write: Missouri Tourism Commission, P.O. Box 1055, 308 E. High St., Jefferson City, Missouri 65101.

Ozark Playgrounds Association is a guide to public parks, many of which have boat ramps and access to boating in southwest Missouri and northwest Arkansas. Information is included on houseboat rentals. Write: Ozark Playgrounds Association, 212 W. 4th St., Joplin, Missouri 64801 (price 50¢).

For *Recreation Opportunities, Federal Power Commission Areas* see entry under Illinois.

For *Quimby's Harbor Guide* see entry under Wisconsin.

NORTH DAKOTA

"Lake Sakakawea" is a map of Corps of Engineer reservoir area coded to list available public recreational facilities and boat ramps. Write: Area Engineer, Garrison Dam, Riverdale, North Dakota 58565.

"Lakes and Reservoirs" is a list of waters where boating is popular, and available facilities. Write: State Outdoor Recreation Agency, State Office Bldg., 900 East Blvd., Bismarck, North Dakota 58501.

OHIO

Ohio River and Tributaries, Small Boat Harbors, Ramps, Landings, etc. is prepared primarily for pleasure craft operators and contains information about facilities and services. Lists names and addresses and

Passengers aboard an aluminum cruiser on the Ohio River near Louisville, Kentucky, experience a remnant of the antebellum days.

telephone numbers of public and commercial marinas to be found along the Ohio River and its tributaries in Ohio and several other states, and gives their location by river mile. The booklet, revised annually, shows availability of fuel and supplies, groceries, overnight moorings, number of berths, and type of launching ramp. Write: U.S. Army Engineer Division, P.O. Box 1159, Cincinnati, Ohio 45201 (price 50¢).

Division Bulletin No. 1, Maps, Charts, Ohio River Division lists charts, maps, and publications considered best suited for pleasure boats in navigating the Ohio River and its tributaries. Write same source as above.

"Boating Facilities and Information Guide for the Wonderful World of Ohio" lists public launching facilities, public lakes, and sources of information for Ohio River and Lake Erie boating. Write: Department of Natural Resources, Division of Watercraft, 1350 Holly Ave., Columbus, Ohio 43212.

"Muskingum River Parkway" gives information on locking through 10 manually operated locks, with map of river parkway and lock and boat launching ramp locations. Write: Ohio Division of Parks & Recreation, 913 Ohio Departments Bldg., Columbus, Ohio 43215.

For *U.S. Lake Survey Chart Catalog of the Great Lakes and Connecting Waters* see entry under Illinois.

SOUTH DAKOTA

Dams, Impoundments, and Reservoirs gives recreational opportunities at three Corps of Engineers' reservoirs along the Missouri River. Each brochure has a map showing public recreation areas, facilities available and accessibility from main roads. Write: U.S. Army Engineer Division, Missouri River, P.O. Box 103, Omaha, Nebraska 68101.

WISCONSIN

"Mississippi River Access Sites" (Dubuque to LaCrosse) lists county locations, names of sites, types of ramps, reverse side is map of site locations. Write: State of Wisconsin, Department of Natural Resources, P.O. Box 450, Madison, Wisconsin 53701.

"Mississippi River Access Sites" (Lacrosse to Prescott) lists locations, ramps, and the like as above. Write same source as above.

Try a Houseboat Vacation gives houseboat specifications, rental rates, conditions, places to visit, and cruise limit areas. Write: Tourist Activities Corp., 112 LaCrosse County Courthouse, LaCrosse, Wisconsin 54601.

"Mississippi Camping and Boating Wonderland" describes launching sites and fuel and grocery docks that are all accessible by water. Write same source as above.

Quimby's Harbor Guide lists all harbor and river towns and marinas for the benefit of boatmen cruising the upper Mississippi River and tributaries; the guide is revised and updated annually. Write: Quimby's Harbor Guide, P.O. Box 85, Prairie du Chien, Wisconsin 53821 (price $2.40).

"Recreation Guide to LaCrosse" is a map coded to show boat landings, marinas, houseboat rentals, and varied recreation. Write: Chamber, City, County Publicity Committee, P.O. Box 842, LaCrosse, Wisconsin 54601.

THE SOUTH CENTRAL AREA

ARKANSAS

Recreation Opportunities at Hydroelectric Projects Licensed by the Federal Power Commission is a booklet showing where recreational facilities exist at hydroelectric power projects in South Central United States. Write: Federal Power Commission, 819 Taylor St., Ft. Worth, Texas 76102.

Arkansas River Waterway, a pamphlet, describes recreational benefits of Corps of Engineers project that provides a navigable channel from the mouth of the Arkansas River to near Tulsa, Oklahoma, a distance of 463 miles. It gives channel dimensions, location of locks, dams, and reservoirs. Write: U.S. Army Corps of Engineers, Little Rock District, P.O. Box 867, Little Rock, Arkansas 72203.

Guidebook to Pleasure Boating on the Arkansas River, a photographic travelog, shows representative scenes along the Arkansas River with public marinas which are pinpointed by river navigation mile. Also given are proper locking, navigation, and mooring procedures. Write: ARKRIV Associates, Inc., P.O. Box 1283, Arkansas Tech, Russellville, Arkansas 72801 (price $2.50).

COLORADO

"Cherry Creek Reservoir" (near Denver, Colorado) map locates recreational facilities including marinas and camp grounds and tells how to get there from major highways. Write: Director, Department of Natural Resources, Division of Game, Fish and Parks, 6060 Broadway, Denver, Colorado 80216.

"Navajo Dam and Lake" is a map of Navajo Lake in Colorado and New Mexico with locations of public use areas and access roads. Tells where there are boat ramps, docks, boat rentals, gasoline, and service. Write same source as above.

KANSAS

State Lake Camping Areas, leaflet shows location of boat ramps administered by the Fish and Game Commission. Write: Forestry, Fish and Game Commission, Information-Education Division, Box 1028, Pratt, Kansas 67124. *Seven Lakes* are pamphlets from the Corps of Engineers describing their multipurpose projects. Map included locates public use areas, recreational facilities and access roads. Write: U.S. Army Corps of Engineers, Kansas City District, 700 Federal Bldg., 601 E. 12th St., Kansas City, Missouri 64106.

LOUISIANA

"List of Free Public Boat Ramps" gives more than 50 ramps, listed alphabetically by parish, showing how to get there by highway. Write: Louisiana Wildlife and Fisheries Commission, Wildlife and Fisheries Bldg., 400 Royal St., New Orleans, Louisiana 70130.

NEBRASKA

"Salt Valley in Nebraska" is a map of 10 Corps of Engineers reservoirs in the Salt Creek Valley around Lincoln, showing surface acreage and access roads. Write: U.S. Army Corps of Engineers, Missouri River Division, Box 103, Downtown Station, Omaha, Nebraska 68101.

"Lewis and Clark Lake" is a map of a lake on Nebraska-South Dakota border indicating facilities available for boating. Write same source as above.

Harlan County Dam and Multiple-Purpose Reservoir includes general information about the multipurpose lake projects, a map locating public use areas, and rules for water safety. Write: U.S. Corps of Engineers,

Houseboaters relax on the Mississippi River near Prairie du Chien, in Crawford County, Wisconsin, a stopover for the early fur traders. (Wis. Natural Resources Dept.)

Kansas City District, 700 Federal Bldg., 601 E. 12th St., Kansas City, Missouri 64106.

Note: The U.S. Army Engineer Division, Missouri River, P.O. Box 103, Downtown Station, Omaha, Nebraska 68101 will furnish an "Information Packet" containing literature about houseboating throughout the Missouri River Basin.

NEW MEXICO

"Boater's Information—Facilities Available at New Mexico State Park Lakes" is a list of lakes and facilities available at each with information on how to get there. Write: New Mexico State Park Commission, P.O. Box 1147, Santa Fe, New Mexico 87501.

For "Navajo Dam and Lake" see entry under Colorado.

OKLAHOMA

Grand Lake of the Cherokees contains boating facilities and regulations for 59,200 acres and 1,300 miles of shoreline, ideal for houseboating 8 months of the year. Write: Grandland Corporation, Box 7569, Grove, Oklahoma 74344.

Arkansas River Waterway, a pamphlet, describes recreational benefits of Corps of Engineers project providing a navigable channel from the mouth of the Arkansas River to Catoosa near Tulsa, Oklahoma. Pamphlet gives channel dimensions and locations of locks, dams and reservoirs. Write: U.S. Army Corps of Engineers, Tulsa District, P.O. Box 61, Tulsa, Oklahoma 74102.

For *Recreation Opportunities at Federal Power Commission Areas* see entry under Arkansas.

TEXAS

"Boat Ramp Locations" lists, county-by-county, location of facilities. Write: Texas Parks & Wildlife Department, Water Safety Services, John H. Reagan Bldg., Austin, Texas 78701.

Lake Texoma pamphlet briefs you on recreational facilities on both the Texas and Oklahoma sides of the lake. Map pinpoints public use areas and access roads, and there is a listing of boating facilities and services available at each site. The navigation aid and marker system used on the reservoir is illustrated. Write: U.S. Army Corps of Engineers, Tulsa District, P.O. Box 61, Tulsa, Oklahoma 74102.

Reclamation's Recreational Opportunities shows Bureau of Reclamation reservoir areas, shoreline miles, available facilities, and administering agencies in Texas and 16 other states. Write: U.S. Department of Interior, Bureau of Reclamation, Region #5, Box 1609, Amarillo, Texas 79105. (Price is 50¢ from Superintendent of Documents, U.S. Printing Office, Washington, D.C. 20402.)

17

The Western Area and
Beyond Our Borders

Boating & Fishing Almanac is a cruising and travel guide for coastal and inland waters of the Pacific Southwest including the Colorado River, Lake Powell, Lake Mead, Salton Sea, the Offshore Channel Islands, Inland Lakes, and the Pacific Coast from Marro Bay to Ensenada. Details are given on harbors, marinas, and launching ramps, plus tide and current tables, star charts, and so on. Write: *Boating & Fishing Almanac*, Box 344, Venice, California 90291 (price $3.60 by mail).

ALASKA
"Alaska Recreation Guide" is a map of Alaska showing recreational facilities maintained by the state and federal agencies. Write: State of Alaska, Division of Parks, 323 E. 4th Ave., Anchorage, Alaska 99501.

Recreation Opportunities at Federal Power Commission Areas, a booklet, shows where recreational facilities and activities exist at FPC-licensed hydroelectric power projects in western United States. Write: Federal Power Commission, 555 Battery St., San Francisco, California 94111.

ARIZONA
"Lake Powell (Glen Canyon National Recreation Area)" is a map of area with description of available facilities and services. Write: Superintendent, Glen Canyon National Recreation Area, Box 1507, Page, Arizona 86040.

For *Recreation Opportunities at Federal Power Commission Areas* see entry under Alaska.

CALIFORNIA

"Boating Recreation in California" maps visually locate boating facilities throughout the state, while accompanying charts give important information about services available. Write: Automobile Club of Southern California, Travel Recreation Department, 2601 S. Figueroa St., Los Angeles, California 94007 (available to AAA members only).

"Guide to Colorado River" is a map of the Colorado River area locating marinas and resort facilities. Write same source as above.

Golden Gate Atlas is a guide to waterways, ports, and facilities of the Central Pacific Coast, Golden Gateway Region. Listed are San Francisco and Pablo Bays' anchorages, ocean routes, and VHF radio channels. Accent is on commercial boating, but there is much here of interest to the houseboater. Write: Marine Exchange, San Francisco Bay Region, 303 World Trade Center, San Francisco, California 94111.

"The William G. Stone Lock, and Your Key to Safe Passage" gives information about the Stone Lock in the Sacramento River Deep Water Ship Channel, with rules and traffic signals for locking through. Write: Department of the Army, Corps of Engineers, 630 Sansome St., Room 1216, San Francisco, California 94111.

"Recreation Plus Marina" lists houseboat rentals, berths, and launching at privately owned facility on Trinity Lake. Write: Shasta-Cascade Wonderland Assoc., P.O. Box 1988, Redding, California 96001.

For *Recreation Opportunities at Federal Power Commission Areas* see entry under Alaska.

Many dams and reservoirs, offering facilities for the houseboater, are scattered throughout the state. They are administered by the Corps of Engineers. For data write: Department of the Army, Corps of Engineers, 630 Sansome St., Room 1216, San Francisco, California 94111.

Information about houseboat rentals for Shasta, Westaire, Aqua, Holiday, Jones Valley, Aqua Cruisers, Digger Bay, Bridge Bay, and Lake Shasta Houseboat Co. on Shasta Lake—rates, layouts to help you choose, equipment furnished, and things to see and do—is available.

Townhouse-style living aboard a Royal Capri is a way of life in sunny California.

Write: Shasta-Cascade Wonderland Assn., P.O. Box 1988, Redding, California 96001.

California's Channel Islands, eight of them, string out for 30 miles along the Southern California Coast. They are dominated by Anacapa, Santa Cruz, Santa Rosa, and San Miguel. The area roughly extends from Santa Barbara to San Clemente, and the water offers ideal cruising for a properly equipped houseboat.

The Delta Region is often called "California's Houseboating Shangri-la." The Sacramento, San Joaquin, and the North and South Forks of the Mokelumne Rivers converge to form an extensive boating playground. Author Erle Stanley Gardner, a houseboat aficionado for many years, through his writings told the Delta story of enjoying the 1,000-mile water course—its marinas, fishing, restaurants, pals, and so on.

Access is available at many marinas and at the towns of Walnut Grove, Stockton, Rio Vista, Locke, and others. Also, state parks in the area offer public ramps for launching, along with the attendant activities of swimming, water skiing, picnicking, and camping. Houseboat rentals are popular, as this ideal drifting water is but an hour or two from the big cities of the Bay area.

HAWAII

"Hawaii Boating Guide" map locates launching ramps, moorages, and service facilities. Also a digest of pleasure boat requirements and illustrations of use of whistle or horn signals, water skiing signals, and storm signals. Write: Union Oil Co. of California, P.O. Box 659, Honolulu, Hawaii 96809.

"Hawaii State Official Transportation Map" contains facts about the state and shows the locations of harbors and other points of interest on the five principal islands. Write: State of Hawaii, Department of Transportation, Harbors Division, P.O. Box 397, Honolulu, Hawaii 96809.

IDAHO

"Reclamation's Recreational Opportunities" is a list of reclamation reservoirs in Idaho and 16 other states showing available facilities, shoreline miles, and so on. Write: U.S. Department of the Interior, Bureau of Reclamation, Region 1, Box 8008, Boise, Idaho 83707. (Price is 20¢ from the Superintendent of Documents, U.S. Printing Office, Washington, D.C. 20402.)

"Albeni Falls Dam, Pend Oreille River" map locates public recreation areas on Lake Pend Oreille in northern Idaho, and lists available boating facilities. Write: U.S. Army Corps of Engineers, Albeni Falls Dam, Box 310, Newport, Washington 99165.

For *Recreation Opportunities at Federal Power Commission Areas* see entry under Alaska.

The Coeur d'Alene area in northern Idaho boasts 50 lakes within a 50-mile radius, offering an endless variety of water, scenery, and challenge. The queen of them all, Coeur d'Alene is rated as one of the 10 most beautiful lakes in the United States. For data write the Chamber of Commerce there.

MONTANA

"Fort Peck Reservoir" is a map of dam and reservoir showing access roads and recreational facilities including boat ramps and docks. Write: U.S. Army Engineer Division, P.O. Box 103, Downtown Station, Omaha, Nebraska 68101.

"Reclamation's Recreational Opportunities" is a list of reservoirs in Montana and 16 other states showing available facilities, shoreline miles, and so on. Write: U.S. Department of the Interior, Bureau of Reclamation, Regional Office, Region 6, Billings, Montana 59103.

For *Recreation Opportunities at Federal Power Commission Areas* see entry under Alaska.

NEVADA

"Lake Mead National Recreation Area" gives suggestions for things to do and see and lists services and facilities along the shores of Lake Mead and Lake Mohave. Write: Lake Mead National Recreation Area, 601 Nevada Highway, Boulder City, Nevada 89005.

For *"Guide to the Colorado River"* see entry under California.

OREGON

Boating in Coastal Waters gives information regarding storm warnings, aids to navigation, charts for coastal waters, U.S. Coast Guard Stations, Auxiliary Patrols, the coastal bars, and recommended safety equipment for boats operating in coastal waters. Write: State Marine Board, State Agricultural Bldg., 635 Capitol St., N.E., Salem, Oregon 97310.

"Oregon Boating Guide" lists launching ramps and related facilities with coded map pinpointing their location and index of lakes and reservoirs, and summarized regulations. Write: Oregon State Highway Division, Travel Information Section, Highway Bldg., Salem, Oregon 97310.

"Steer a Course to the Port of Coos Bay" from the Charleston Boat Basin, administered by the Port of Coos Bay, gives moorage rates. Write: Charleston Boat Basin, Box 409, Charleston, Oregon 97420.

For *Recreation Opportunities at Federal Power Commission Areas* see entry under Alaska.

20 Areas: Dams, Locks, Reservoirs, brochures, are available, describing the locks, dams reservoirs areas, coastal harbors, and navigation channels constructed and operated by the Corps of Engineers in Oregon and along the Oregon-Washington boundary. They include maps locating public use and access areas. Write: Department of the Army, Corps of Engineers, Portland District, P.O. Box 2946, Portland, Oregon 97208.

UTAH

"River Guides and Outfitters" lists guides and outfitters operating in the state who have excellent records of satisfying their customers. Write: Utah Travel Council, Council Hall, Salt Lake City, Utah 84114.

"Recreation on Reclamation Lakes, Region 4" lists recreation areas and the kind of facilities available on Reclamation reservoirs in Utah and other states. Write: Bureau of Reclamation, Region 4 Office, P.O. Box 11568, Salt Lake City, Utah 84111.

The Rainbow Marina offers houseboaters easy access to one of Lake Powell's major attractions, Rainbow National Monument. (Utah Travel Council Photo)

For *Recreation Opportunities at Federal Power Commission Areas* see entry under Alaska.

Lake Powell (Glen Canyon National Recreation Area) gives all the information needed to houseboat on this midnight-blue water with a shoreline that is the longest in the West: marinas, points of access, rentals, answers to every question. See entry under Arizona.

WASHINGTON

"Cruising Information Kit" provides a wealth of information about safety afloat. Also included are a chart of Tacoma, Lower Puget Sound and the Lower Hood Canal showing facilities for the small boater and a pamphlet describing recreational boating facilities of Washington ports. Write: Tacoma *News Tribune,* 711 St. Helens Ave., Tacoma, Washington 98402.

"Recreational Boating Facilities of Washington Ports" is a list and coded map of harbors operated by public ports. Details of facilities and services available: dry storage, moorage, launch lift, rates too. Write: Washington Ports Association, 210 East Union Ave., P.O. Box 1518, Olympia, Washington 98501.

"Guidelines for Boaters Using Lake Washington Ship Canal and Hiram Chittenden Locks" tells you the proper way to use the locks and canal. Write U.S. Army Corps of Engineers, Chittenden Locks, 3015 N.W. 54th St., Seattle, Washington 98107.

"Lower Monumental Lock and Dam" is a map showing four major multiple-public-benefit dam-and-lock projects under construction which will extend shallow-draft navigation as far inland as the Washington-Idaho line. Write U.S. Army Corps of Engineers, Bldg. 602, City-County Airport, Walla Walla, Washington 99362.

"McNary Lock and Dam-Columbia River" gives reservoir information with map showing boat ramp locations and marinas, plus rules of the road, illustrations of navigation aids, and how to request lockage. Write above source.

For *Recreation Opportunities at Federal Power Commission Areas* see entry under Alaska.

WYOMING

"Family Water Sports in Big Wyoming" is a chart systematically listing the water bodies in the state that lie in the national parks, national forests, state parks, and also by drainage. Rivers, streams, lakes, and reservoirs can be pinpointed by using the map coordinates. Write: Wyoming Travel Commission, 2320 Capitol Ave., Cheyenne, Wyoming 82001.

BEYOND OUR BORDERS

CANADA

So You're Going to Canada, a booklet, gives tips on crossing the border without difficulty or delay, declaration of equipment, operation of radio equipment, and the amount of goods you can bring back from Canada duty-free. Write: Canadian Government Travel Bureau, Ottawa, Canada.

"Quebec Cruising the Waterways" lists yachting harbors, marinas, launching and docking facilities, and services available at each along Quebec waterways. Write: Province of Quebec, Department of Tourism, 930 Chemin Sainte-Foy, Quebec, Canada.

Ontario Boating is a picturesque booklet listing cruising areas, marine facilities, boat repairs, general services, ship-to-shore radio facilities, and points of interest along Ontario's waterways. Write Department of Tourism, Province of Ontario, Parliament Buildings, Toronto, Canada.

"Navigation Canals" offers cruising information for boatmen who wish to use the canal systems of Canada. Literature contains mileage, canal regulations, aids to navigation, signals for locks and bridges, lock dimensions, clearance papers, and so forth. Write: Department of Transport, Ottawa, Canada.

British Columbia Tourist Directory includes names, locations, and facilities provided by the marine parks. Also there's a guide to launching sites, fishing camps, and resorts. Write: British Columbia Department of Travel Industry, Parliament Buildings, Victoria, British Columbia, Canada.

Manitoba Vacation Handbook gives information about Manitoba's vacation areas. All boat-launching sites are grouped under four geographic regions and indicate highway access. Write Tourist Branch, Department of Tourism and Recreation, 408-401 York Ave., Winnipeg 1, Manitoba, Canada.

"Saskatchewan Travel Guide" is a complete listing of facilities at regional parks that offer boating. Write: Tourist Development Branch, Power Bldg., Regina, Saskatchewan, Canada.

From Sicamous, British Columbia, touted as the "Houseboat Capital of Canada" across the sweep of provinces to the Atlantic Ocean, you'll find a bit, and more, of what you are looking for.

Appendix

ASSOCIATIONS

■ **Boating Industry Associations (BIA),** 401 N. Michigan Ave., Chicago, Illinois 60611.

Serving as a watchdog of the industry, the BIA helps both the manufacturer and customer. BIA certification is given to houseboat models that meet federal requirements and their own standards.

■ **Boat Owners Association of the United States,** 1028 Connecticut Ave., Washington, D.C. 20036.

The following services are made available to members: chart and map service, boat financing plan, book and magazine discounts, correspondence course on seamanship and piloting, boat theft and vandalism protection program, cruise planning aid, and other aids. *Boat/U.S. Reports* is published monthly; subscription: $4.

■ **Houseboat Association of America,** P.O. Box 7285, Asheville, North Carolina 28807.

Association offers to members the special services needed by houseboat enthusiasts and owners, ranging from the home-built unit to the owner of the most palatial craft manufactured. Services are varied and extensive: charting for planned trips; free subscription to *Family Houseboating* magazine; bimonthly *Newsletter* with the latest information on new products, legislation, and news of members; an insurance program; discounts on rentals; and other services. Membership fee is $15 annually.

■ **Marine Accessories and Services Association,** 401 N. Michigan Ave., Chicago, Illinois 60611.

Information is available on sources of the complete range of accessories, optional items, interior and exterior appointments, and safety equipment.

■ **Outboard Boating Club of America (OBC),** 401 N. Michigan Ave., Chicago, Illinois 60611.

OBC offers free of charge such publications as *Use of Common Sense Afloat, Launching Ramps and Piers, Facilities File,* and many other services.

MAGAZINES

■ **Family Houseboating,** P.O. Box 500, Calabasas, California 91302, Denis M. Rouse, Editorial Director.

The only magazine devoted exclusively to houseboating, it has an excellent staff covering the houseboating scene: evaluation of models, rentals, areas of participation, engine care and maintenance, galley and menu information, navigation data, legislation, and many personal experiences. Your first step in the houseboating adventure is to subscribe at $4 a year.

■ **Motor Boating & Sailing,** 224 W. 57th St., New York, New York 10019, John R. Whiting, Publisher.

This is an old-line, solid publication that carries information on the broader phases of boating. The houseboater can use to good advantage much of its content.

Other worthy magazines are noted. Read a few, and see if your needs are met by their content.

■ **Boat and Motor Dealer,** 829 Main St., Evanston, Illinois 60202.

■ **Boating Industry Magazine,** 205 E. 42nd St., New York, New York 10017.

■ **Lakeland Boating,** 412 Longshore Dr., Ann Arbor, Michigan 48107.

■ **Rudder Magazine,** 1515 Broadway, New York, New York 10024.

■ **Sea & Pacific Motor Boat,** P.O. Box 20227, Long Beach, California 90801.

BOOKS

■ **Piloting Seamanship & Small Boat Handling,** by Charles F. Chapman, 959 8th Ave., New York, New York 10019.

The acknowledged authority on subjects relating to all phases of boating, this "bible of boating" offers the newest developments in the field.

The book includes a complete, illustrated course prepared especially to develop skill, pleasure, and safety in the navigation of small boats on our waters.

■ **The Ship's Medicine Chest and First Aid at Sea.** Write Superintendent of Documents, Government Printing Office, Washington, D.C. 20402.

■ **First Aid Manual,** and **Life Saving & Water Safety,** both by the American Red Cross, are obtainable from your local chapter.

BOAT TRAINING COURSES

The Coast Guard indicates that only 20 percent of current boatmen had ever been reached by formal boating education courses. The houseboater, investing a goodly sum in his craft, should become knowledgeable in all phases of boating for the safety of all aboard and protection of his investment.

■ **The U.S. Coast Guard Auxiliary Boating Instruction.** Free public education courses in boating safety and seamanship are offered by experienced and qualified Auxiliary members. The courses are designed for both the beginner who wants to acquire basic knowledge of boating and for the more experienced boatman who would like to review the fundamentals. Three separate courses are offered:

1. Outboard Motorboat Handling (1 lesson). The main emphasis is on safety, and practices that all outboard owners should know.
2. Safe Boating (3 lessons). This course provides the elements of seamanship, aids to navigation, rules of the road, and boating safety.
3. Basic Seamanship (8 lessons). This complete course covers the rules of the road, aids to navigation, piloting, safe motorboat operation, and boating laws. A certificate is awarded upon completion of the course.

■ **United States Power Squadron.** This nation-wide association of boatmen conducts an extensive program of instruction. The local squadrons throughout the country present a basic course of 12 lectures, known as the Piloting Course, which is open to all enthusiasts.

FIRST-AID TRAINING

At least one member of every crew should have, as a proper background skill to boating, a knowledge of first-aid practices. The American Red Cross gives a beginner's and advanced course free of charge. Many accidents asea require immediate attention, and treatments of various injuries have changed in light of new discoveries, all of which prove that first-aid treatment knowledge is necessary.

SOURCES OF SUPPLY

The addresses of companies mentioned in the preceding pages are here noted. The list is not, by far, comprehensive, nor are many other excellent sources noted for lack of space.

■ **James Bliss & Co.,** 100 Route 128, Denham, Massachusetts 02026.

■ **Bremer Mfg. Co.,** Box 548, Elkhart Lake, Wisconsin 53020.

■ **Coleman Co. Inc.,** Wichita, Kansas 67201.

■ **Danforth,** 500 Riverside Industrial Pkwy., Portland, Maine 04103.

■ **Lowrance Electronics Mfg. Corp.,** 12000 E. Skelly Dr., Tulsa, Oklahoma 74128.

■ **Jerry Martin Co.,** 4411 Grand Ave., Gurnee, Illinois 60031.

■ **Sears, Roebuck & Co.,** 303 E. Ohio St., Dept. 703, Chicago, Illinois 60611.

■ **N. A. Taylor Co.,** Gloverville, New York 12078.

■ **Thermos Division,** Norwich, Connecticut 06360.

■ **Vorta Systems, Inc.,** Box 613, Round Lake, Illinois 60073.

Index

Abaft, 32
Abeam, 32
Alabama, 137, 153
Alarm systems, 71
Alaska, 169
Aluminum Cruisers, Inc., 96–97
Aluminum hulls, 24, 27
Americana Living Cruisers, 97
Anchors, 56–58, 75
Arizona, 144, 169–70
Arkansas, 142, 166
Army Corps of Engineers, U.S., 62
Army Engineer District, U.S., 43
Auxiliary craft, 66

Babies on houseboats, 87
Ball, Pete, 22
Barges, 62–63
Barometers, 75
Bastis, Tom, 22
Beach, David D., 8
Beaching, 66–67
Bell buoys, 36, 47
Bells, 75
Berths, 31
Bilge, 33
Binnacles, 36
Binoculars, 75
Bird watching, 92–93
Boat and Motor Dealer, 176
Boatel Co., Inc., 97–98
Boat hooks, 75

Boating Almanac, 148
Boating & Fishing Almanac, 169
Boating Industry Association, 22, 32, 52, 53, 55, 175
Boating Industry Magazine, 176
Boating Safety Advisory Council, 54
Boat Owners Association of the United States, 175
Boat racks, 64
Boat Safety Act, Federal, 52–54, 74
  aid to distressed boats required by, 67, 78
Boat training courses, 177
Broaching, 39
Brooks, Dick, 22
Buoys, 36, 44–47
Burden (right of way), 36, 50–51
Burns Craft, 98–99
Byquist, Jack, 22

California, 144, 170–71
Canada,
  houseboating waters in, 174
  houseboat rentals in, 145
Can buoys, 36, 44
Capacity plate, 76
Caribbean, houseboat rentals in, 134, 145
Carri-Craft, Inc., 99
Catamaran, 33
Cat's cradle (game), 85–86
Certificate of Number, 74

Chapman, Charles F., 176–77
Charts (maps), 41–43
Cherry Grove (Fire Island, N.Y.), 13
Chicago (Illinois), 13
Children on houseboats, 82–87
Chine, 33
Chittenden Lock (Washington), 59
Chocks, 33
Chris-Craft Industries, Inc., 100–1
Cleaning supplies, 71–73
Clearwater (Florida), 18
Cleat, 33
Coastal Warning Facilities Charts, 49
Coast and Geodetic Survey, U.S., 42
Coast Guard, U.S., 120
  auxiliary boating instruction by, 177
  bouyage system of, 44
  defect notification by, 28
  equipment and numbering requirements of, 71, 74
  rules of the road and, 51–54
Coco Lobo (Nixon's houseboat), 13
Colorado, 166–67
Compass, 73
Competitive houseboating, 18
Connecticut, 148

Construction of houseboats, 24
Cooking facilities, 82–83, 95
Coolers, 76
Corps of Engineers, U.S., 62
Cross-Florida Boat-A-Cade, 18
Cutter (Division of Cargile, Inc.), 124–25

Danforth and Northill anchors, 56, 75
Davits, 33
Day beacons, 47
Deck lines, 73
    see also Ropes
Delaware, 136
Depth, measurement of, 41–42
Depth sounders, 76
Dinghies, 34, 63, 66
District of Columbia, 136
Docking, 64–65
    fees, 10
Dogs on houseboats, 88–89
Dry rot, 34

Echols, Don, 22
Electrolytic damage to hulls, 24, 27
Engine control, 26–27
Engineering standards for houseboats, 22
Engines, 25–27
    spare parts for, 77
Environmental Protection Agency (U.S.), 55
Equipment, 71–80
Erie Canal (N.Y.), 61
Europe, houseboat rentals in, 145

Family Houseboating, 176
Federal Boat Safety Act, 52–54, 74
    aid to distressed boats required by, 67, 68
Fenders, 34, 58, 64, 65, 77
Fiberglass hulls, 24, 27, 34
Fire extinguishers, 73
First-Aid kit, 77–78

First Aid Manual, 177
First-Aid training, 177
Fishing, 16, 92
Flame arresters, 73
Flares, 78–79
Floating Chapel, 12
Floating homes, 119–24
Florida, 137–38, 153–55
Flotation, 34
Flying bridges, 79
Ft. Lauderdale (Florida), 18
Foul weather gear, 79
Fume detectors, 73

Galleys, 82–83, 95
Georgia, 138, 155–56
Georgian Steel Boats, Ltd., 101
Glendale Plastics, 125–26
Glen L. Marine Designs, 133
Gong buoys, 47
Gunkholing, 14
Gunwale, 34

Hadley, Paul, 22
Harbor House Corp., 101–3
Hawaii, 144, 171
Hawsers, 34
Heads (toilets), 34, 80, 95
Holiday Mansion, 103–4
Hoover, Herbert, 13
Horns, 75
Horsepower, 26
Houseboat Association of America, 175
Houseboat Bank, 12–13
Houseboats,
    floating homes as, 119–24
    models of, 94–118
    pontoon boats as, 129–33
    rentals of, 134–45
    requirements of, 8–10
    selecting, 19–30
    trailerable, 124–28
    used, 27–28, 53

Huck Finn, Inc., 133
Hulls, 23–24, 27
Hunting, 16

Idaho, 143, 171
Illinois, 140, 160–62
Inboard diesel engines, 26
Inboard engines, 25–26
Inboard-outboard engines, 25, 35
Indiana, 140–41, 162
Inland Rules of the Road, 50
Insurance, 30
Intercoms, 79
International Houseboat Manufacturer's Association, 22
International Rules of the Road, 50
Iowa, 141, 162

James, Russ, 22

Kansas, 142, 167
Kayot, Inc., 131
Kayot Marine Division, 104–5
Keels, 35
Kennedy Houseboats, Inc., 126, 133
Kentucky, 141, 162
Key Biscayne (Florida), 13
Key Largo (Florida), 13
King's Craft, 105–7
Knots, 68–70

Ladders, 79
Lakeland Boating, 176
Lazy-Days Manufacturing Co., Inc., 107–8
Life Saving & Water Safety, 177
Lifesaving devices, 73
Lighted buoys, 47
Light requirements, 73–74
Limburg, Al, 55
Lines, *see* Ropes
Locks (waterway), 58–62
Long Beach (California), 120

Lore, Ray, 55, 122
Louisiana, 142, 167

Macerator-chlorinator, 55
MacMinn, Ney, 93
McGowan, Seabury, 22
Maine, 136, 148
Manila ropes, 68
Maps (charts), 41–43
Marinas, 86, 92
Marine Accessories and Services Association, 176
Maryland, 136, 149
Maurell Products, Inc., 108–9
Massachusetts, 136, 149
Maxa Industries, Inc., 109
Megaphones, 79
Miami (Florida), 14
Miami River (Florida), 14
Michigan, 141, 162–64
Midwestern region of U.S., houseboating waters in, 159–66
houseboat rentals in, 140–42
Minnesota, 141–42, 164
Mississippi, 139, 156
Mississippi River, 159–60
Missouri, 142–43, 164
Mobile Cruising Guides, 148
Mobil Safety Afloat, 147–48
MonArk Boat Co., 109
Montana, 172
Moorings, 63–64
Motor Boat Act (U.S.), 71
Motor Boating & Sailing, 176
Motors, 25–27
Mushroom anchors, 56, 75

National Weather Service, U.S., 49
Nauta-Line, Inc., 110–11
Nautical rules of the road, 50–55
Naval Oceanographic Office, U.S., 42–43
Navigation, 43–47
Nebraska, 143, 167–68
Nevada, 172

New Hampshire, 136, 149
New Jersey, 136
New Mexico, 168
New York, 136–37, 149–50
New York Barge Canal, 61
New York City (N.Y.), 13
Nichols, Glen, 22
Nixon, Richard M., 13
North Carolina, 139, 156
North Central region of U.S., houseboating waters in, 159–66
houseboat rentals in, 140–42
North Dakota, 164
Northeastern region of U.S., houseboating waters in, 147–51
houseboat rentals in, 135–37
Northwestern region of U.S., houseboating waters in, 169–74
houseboat rentals in, 143
Numbering requirements, 74
Nun buoys, 37, 44
Nylon ropes, 67, 68, 73

Ohio, 142, 164–65
Oklahoma, 143, 168
Oregon, 143, 172
Outboard Boating Club of America, 147, 176
Outboard motors, 25
Overnight trips, 18

Pacemaker Corp., 111
Papa's Restaurant (Florida), 92
Paris (France), 93
Pennsylvania, 150
Pensacola (Florida), 16
Peterson, Dick, 22
Pier 66 Franchised Marina Directory, 147
Piloting Seamanship & Small Boat Handling (Chapman), 176–77
Pioneer Lake Lutheran Church Conover (Wisconsin), 12
Pontoon boats, 129–33
Portofino (California), 120–21

Privilege (right of way), 38, 50–51
Puget Sound (Washington), 14
Pumps, 74

Quimby's Harbor Guide, 160

Radar, 79
Radios, 79
Rear-view mirrors, 79
Registration, boat, 10
Rentals of houseboats, 134–45
Retirement, 90–93
Rhode Island, 150
Right of way, 50–51
River Queen, 112
Ropes (lines), 68, 73, 79
towing, 67
Rudder Magazine, 176
Rules of the road, nautical, 50–55

Sacramento River (California), 120
Safety equipment, 71–75
Sanpon Boats, 133
Sausalito (California), 120
Scuba diving, 14–16
Sea & Pacific Motor Boat, 176
Sea Camper, 126–27
SeaLine Boats, Inc., 112–13
Sea Rover Marine, 113–14
Sears, Roebuck & Co., 131
Seastrom, Jack, 22
Seattle (Washington), 14
Security National Bank (N.Y.), 12–13
Seine River (France), 93
Sheathing, 35
Ship's Medicine Chest and First Aid at Sea, The, 177
Slip moorings, 64
Snorkeling, 14–16
Sound buoys, 47
Sources of Waterway Information, 147
South Carolina, 139, 156–57

South Central region of U.S.,
    houseboating waters in, 166–68
    houseboat rentals in, 142–43
South Dakota, 165
Southeastern region of U.S.,
    houseboating waters in, 153–58
    houseboat rentals in, 137–39
South Sea Islands, 85
Southwestern region of U.S.,
    houseboating waters in, 169–74
    houseboat rentals in, 144
Spar buoys, 47
Spare fuel tanks, 74
Spare parts, 77
Speed, 39
Speedometers, 79
Sport-Craft, 114
Stardust Cruiser Mfg. Co., 114–15
Star gazing, 18
Steel hulls, 24, 27
Steury Corp., 127
St. Lawrence Waterway, 59
Stone, Ron, 55
Stringers, 35
Supplies, sources of, 178
Swimming, 85
Sylvan Industries, Inc., 131

Tennessee, 139, 157–58
Tents, 79
Texas, 143, 168
Toilets (heads), 34, 80, 95
Tool kits, 80
Towboats, 62–63
Towing, 67–68
Trailerable houseboats, 124–28
Trailering, 64, 124
Trail or Float Corp., 127–28
Transfer of number, 74
Transom, 35
Trollers, 80
Twain, Mark, 159

Uniflite, Inc., 115–17
United States Coast Pilot, 47
United States Power Squadron, 177
Used houseboats, 27–28, 53
Utah, 143, 172–73

Ventilators, 75
Vermont, 151
V-hulls, 23, 35
Virginia, 139, 158

Warranties, 30

Washington, 143, 173–74
Waste discharge, 54–55
Watercraft, Inc., 117
Water Quality Improvement Act
    (U.S.), 54–55
Water skiing, 18, 62–63
Waterway Guide, 148
Wedding receptions on houseboats,
    13
Western region of U.S.,
    houseboating waters in, 169–74
    houseboat rentals in, 143–44
West Virginia, 139, 158
Whipping rope, 70
Whistle buoys, 47
Whistles, 75
Whitcraft Houseboat Division of
    AMF, 117–18
Whittaker, Dick, 22
Wind warning signals, 47–49
Wisconsin, 142, 166
Wood hulls, 24
Wyoming, 174

Yachtsman's anchors, 56
Yachtster, Inc., 128
Yukon-Delta, Inc., 128